VIEWS
of
LOUISVILLE
since
1766

2.

VIEWS
of
LOUISVILLE
since
1766

SAMUEL W. THOMAS, *Editor*

Introduction by BARRY BINGHAM, SR.

Contents

PREFACE

Views of Louisville since 1766 is an outgrowth of the Barry Bingham family's continuing interest in visual communication and their efforts to support and encourage the newly founded Photographic Archives of the University of Louisville. Established in 1968, this regional photographic depository has already acquired collections of noteworthy size and significance. One such collection contains the photographs of Louisville amassed by R. G. Potter and obtained for the Archives from a grant by *The Courier-Journal and Louisville Times.*

It was originally planned to publish early photographs of Louisville in a small pictorial booklet, to focus attention on the important collections in our community's rapidly growing photographic repository. However, preliminary examination of these early photographs revealed that the city's transition from a rawboned frontier town to a burgeoning river community preceeded popular use of the camera, and that photographic art alone could not convey the full flavor of Louisville's past. A decision was made to enlarge the size of the publication, incorporating the legacy of all types of pictorial material, including sketches, paintings and engravings. It was felt that adding these essentially earlier forms of illustration would not only provide a view of the infant community but would give an additional dimension and continuity to the later photographs.

Views of Louisville since 1766 is not in the strictest sense a pictorial history. Pictures have not been included to illustrate a preconceived arrangement of dates or events. Rather, they have, by their multiple relationships to each other, created their own text. Generally, the illustrations fall into chronological order and are grouped to reveal the scenes contemporaries focused on most frequently, a mirror of the issues — economic growth or religious revival, social reform or political ferment — which preoccupied the illustrators. But when more recent illustrations would provide an added perspective or interesting contrast, they have been interposed.

The reflections and descriptions excerpted from contemporary writings are not firmly bound to particular illustrations. They are merely additional illustrations, word pictures, and evoke their own visual impression in the mind. To prevent the illustrations from being cluttered with what might seem superfluous information, an appendix section, Notes and Credits, compartmentalizes the provenance of each item, providing as much pertinent data as extensive research could uncover. Particular emphasis was placed upon research into when the illustration was made and whether it was published. All the data is keyed in the Notes and Credits section by page and an assigned number.

The work of editing a pictorial book falls principally into two categories. One must first locate, document and systematically arrange significant illustrations. Secondly, and equally important, it is necessary to supply the printer with copy photographs of uniform quality, a seemingly overwhelming task in view of the variety of sizes, shapes, physical conditions and locations in which the original illustrations are found. Equal to this difficult undertaking was my friend and colleague, Dr. Ernest M. Ellison, director of Instructional Television at the University of Louisville's Health Sciences Center. I have seen him work hours with just one negative to bring out every detail in the final print. His helpful suggestions, quiet confidence, continued excitement and hours of darkroom time have been the mainstay of this project.

The selection of Osmond S. Guy, former director of the Louisville School of Art, to design the book was a stroke of good fortune. We agreed at the outset to make *Views of Louisville since 1766* essentially a visual experience. Oz, constantly chiding me about my fear of too much negative space, accomplished our objective with a simple, straightforward and unencumbered format. His patience and perseverance brought us through many trying evenings at his drawing board, and his talent speaks for itself on the following pages.

Samuel W. Thomas

6.

ACKNOWLEDGMENTS

I am indebted to many persons who helped this project during its year and a half existence. Each contributor's assistance was essential to the completeness and significance of the resulting compilation. Because pictures can be classified in so many ways, few attempts have been made to catalogue whole collections. Consequently, most picture searches must be conducted item by item, requiring an extra effort. I am certain my requests overtaxed the patience of many curators and research assistants, and I am most grateful for their informative responses, which I will acknowledge later.

On my first visit to the Prints and Photographs Division of the Library of Congress, a knowledgeable looking fellow took a second from his hectic research to inquire what I was hunting for. "Louisville, huh? Let me see what I can find." He returned with several uncatalogued birds-eye views of Louisville, items, whose whereabouts he knew from his thirty years of experience servicing the Library's print collection. Before the week was out, Milton Kaplan, curator of historical prints, had demonstrated again and again the necessity of returning to the Library of Congress with time to examine the multitude of uncatalogued collections, made up mostly of items sent to the Library for copyright. Upon my return, I enjoyed the rare privilege of unbridled access to the thousands of pictorial items contained on the Library's closed decks. As an author of several pictorial books himself, Milt Kaplan had plenty of enthusiastic advice for this novice, and he continued to call my attention to Louisville items as he discovered them. He has simply been an essential element in this book's makeup. I would also like to acknowledge the helpful assistance of Milt's colleagues, Renata V. Shaw, Jerry L. Kearns and Walter W. Ristow, chief of the Geography and Maps Division.

I am equally indebted to the following individuals representing public institutions and those owning private collections who supplied pictures or information. Georgia B. Bumgardner, curator of maps and prints, American Antiquarian Society, Worcester, Mass.; James B. Calvert, Louisville; Lee Jordan, librarian, The Cincinnati Historical Society; Thomas G. Addison, librarian, Rare Book Room, The Public Library of Cincinnati and Hamilton County; Marie Czach, assistant curator for photography, The Art Institute of Chicago; Margaret McFadden, assistant curator for manuscripts and archives, special collections, The Joseph Regenstein Library, University of Chicago; Shirley N. Alley, photographs department, The State Historical Society of Colorado, Denver; Robin Cooper, Jr., Louisville; Linda Heaton, registrar, Detroit Historical Commission; Robert J. Doherty, director, Allen R. Hite Art Institute, University of Louisville; Robert A. Sobieszek, curatorial assistant, George Eastman House, Rochester, N.Y.; Gail Freckleton, Eastman Kodak Company, Rochester, N.Y.; Ernest M. Ellison, Louisville; Elisabeth L. Flynn, Longwood College, Farmville, Va.; Waldemar H. Fries, Providence, R.I.; William F. Furnish, Louisville; Carolyn E. Jakeman, The Houghton Library, Harvard University, Cambridge, Mass.; Hubert H. Hawkins, director, Indiana Historical Bureau, Indianapolis; George Raleigh Jewell, Louisville; Anne McDonnell, librarian, Kentucky Historical Society, Frankfort; Clay Lancaster, Brooklyn, N.Y.; Lillian Tonkin, reference librarian; The Library Company of Philadelphia; Vassilia Moore, LIFE, New York; Edison H. Thomas, manager, News Bureau, Louisville & Nashville Railroad Company; Margaret M. Bridwell and Elizabeth D. Byrne, former librarians, Art Library, University of Louisville; R. Fairleigh Lussky, Louisville; Donald E. MacGregor, Louisville; Lois B. McCauley, curator of graphics, Maryland Historical Society, Baltimore; Iva Louise McElwain, Louisville; Douglas W. Marshall, head, map and print division, William L. Clements Library, University of Michigan, Ann Arbor; Ruth K. Field, curator, pictorial history gallery, Missouri Historical Society, St. Louis; W. Sidney Park, Louisville; John D. Kilbourne, curator. The Historical Society of Pennsylvania, Philadelphia; Josephine Motylewski, Charles Thomas and Paul White, National Archives and Records Service, Washington, D.C.; Kenneth M. Newman, New York; James J. Heslin, director, The New-York Historical Society, New York; R. G. Potter, Louisville; Martin F. Schmidt, librarian, Kentucky Room, Louisville Free Public Library; A. Franklin Page, director and Mary E. Carver, registrar, The J. B. Speed Art Museum, Louisville; Adolph Stuber, Rochester, N.Y.; William J. Van Schreevan, state archivist, Virginia State Library, Richmond; R. Haven Wiley, New York; George H. Yater, Louisville.

The staffs of the Library and News Photography Department of The Courier-Journal • The Louisville Times, the Photographic Archives of the University of Louisville, directed by John Church, and The Filson Club provided this project with continued support. I appreciate having had ready access to their collections.

Finally, I am very grateful to James R. Bentley and Evelyn E. Gordinier of Louisville and L. Diane Sawyer of Washington, D.C. for valuable and necessary editing assistance.

7.

8.

INTRODUCTION

What makes a city like no other city, but positively and continuously itself? What is the peculiar genius of the place, the quality that influences all who live there and shapes the changing forces of its destiny?

Those like myself who have lived in Louisville all our lives have an image of the community clearly in our minds, a mosaic pattern of memories collected since childhood. But do we have any vision of what Louisville looked like when our grandfathers and great-grandfathers walked these streets? And can a newcomer to our old town penetrate behind the facade of today and discover the underlying structure of yesterday and of all the many days before?

These are questions of the kind that inspired the publication of *Views of Louisville since 1766*. It is not a formal history. It is instead a set of graphic impressions of a certain town in a certain place through the years.

We all know why Louisville was founded at this particular spot. A member of George Croghan's expedition in 1766 remarked on the character of this sweep of the Ohio, on "the beautiful stillness of the river's course above the rapids."

We know that our official history began with an act of the Virginia legislature in May, 1780: "Whereas sundry inhabitants of the County of Kentucky have, at great expense and hazard, settled themselves on certain lands at the Falls of the Ohio, . . . the same is hereby established as a town by the name of Louisville."

We know that the site of the settlement was a sort of natural crossroads, a point where animals from prehistoric times had moved across the river plain, where migratory birds marked their uncharted voyages through the air, where men seemed destined to congregate.

What we want to know more and more, as we study the bare facts of Louisville's history, is the look of the place as seen through the eyes of generations of travellers and settlers.

We can conjure up the scene at that first Christmas celebration at Fort-on-Shore in 1778, when John Donne's servant Cato Watts played the fiddle right merrily; but can we envision the surroundings of the tiny settlement, "the encroaching forests inhabited by bears, panthers, wolves and wildcats?" By 1828, Captain Basil Hall was able to comment on the beauty and not the danger of those surrounding woodlands: "The trees around Louisville are incomparably finer than any we have seen elsewhere, especially the sycamores."

We would dearly like to know the exact look of the tract of land that John Campbell and John Connolly proposed to sell off in lots for the price of four Spanish dollars each. We would like to share what that keen observer, John James Audubon, and his wife Lucy beheld when they drifted into Louisville on a flatboat in 1808. We long for a glimpse of that same waterfront when Captain Nicholas Roosevelt piloted the first steamboat to make a landing here, on a still, moonlit night in the October of 1811, and when his revolutionary craft issued such a blast of steam that the whole town jumped out of bed and rushed to the wharf, thinking a comet had fallen into the river.

We are eager to look at Louisville through the eyes of a long succession of visitors: Charles Dickens, elegantly installed at the Galt House in 1842; the excited viewers of the first Kentucky Derby in 1875; the strolling tourists, the top-hatted men and the ladies in their swaying bustles, at the Southern Exposition in 1883.

The physical aspect of Louisville through all the years of its growth is fascinating to contemplate. As Thucydides observed more than two millenia ago, however, "it is men who make a city, not walls or ships." We want to look into the faces of past generations of Louisvillians, including most particularly their children. Do they show some subtle overall resemblance, a kind of community look which we can still identify today?

Sam Thomas has sought to satisfy our curiosity about our municipal past, as far as the most diligent research into old records and pictorial documents will allow. The task could never have been undertaken without the Photographic Archives established at the University of Louisville.

Dr. Thomas' book will, I believe, enrich any reader's understanding of the Louisville so many of us love, but so imperfectly know.

Barry Bingham, Sr.

MAPPING THE DEVELOPMENT 1766-1829

The Floods that accompanied us many Days, left us at Sioto, and we found the Water at the Falls low. The Falls ought not to be called so, as the Stream on the North Side has no Sudden Pitch, but only runs rapid over the Ledge of a flat Limestone Rock, which the Author of Nature has put there to keep up the Waters of the higher Ohio; and to be the Cause of that beautiful Stillness of the Rivers Course above it. That this bed or Dam should not wear it is made almost flat and Smooth to resist less the current, which would sooner get the better of greater Resistances, but as it is still subject to wear, there is made enough of it, being two Miles wide, and its Length into the Country on each Side, as covered with Soil, unknown. Mr [George] Morgan unloaded one third and with the assistance of the Indians who knew the Channel best & were usefull and willing, got his Boats safe down The Rapid on the N. side. The carrying Place is 3 Qrtrs. of a Mile on this Side & half as much on the S.E. This last is safer for those that are unacquainted, but more tedious, as during Part of the Summer and fall they must drag their Boats over the Flat Rock. Had we continued with the Flood we should have had no carrying at all. The Companys Boats that passed in April were not sensible of any Falls neither knew the Place where they are. In the course of Communication a Serjs Post will be necessary & useful here. The Situation of it will be mark'd on the Plan.

Harry Gordon, June 1766.

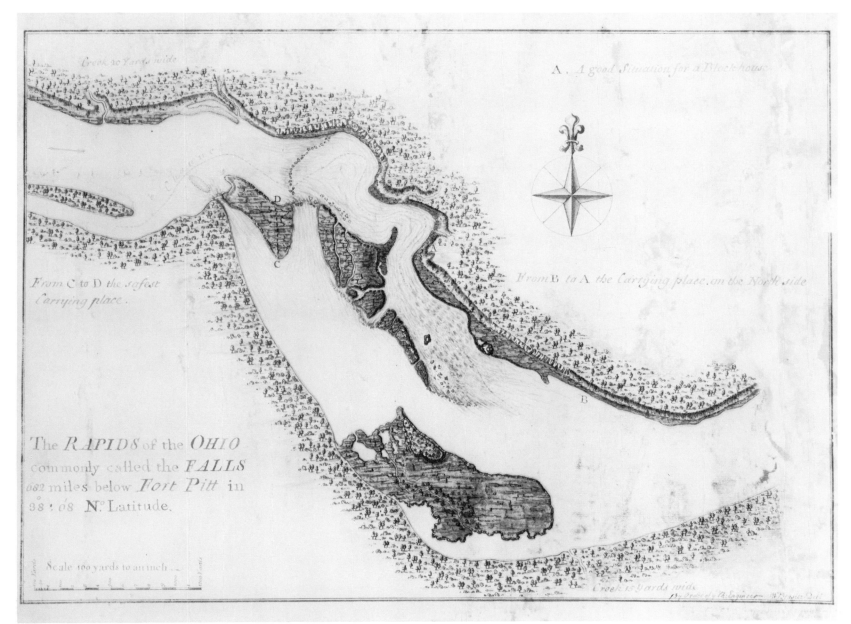

First map of Falls of the Ohio area by William Brasier who accompanied George Croghan's expedition from Fort Pitt to the Illinois country in 1766. Beargrass "Creek 15 Yards wide," noted at bottom, entered the Ohio between 3rd and 4th Streets before rerouted.

12.

Pittsburgh trader John Campbell owned part of Louisville site.

2.

John Connolly was granted 2000 acres at Falls by Lord Dunmore.

3.

THE Subscribers, Patentees of Land at the Falls of the *Ohio*, hereby inform the Publick that they intend to lay out a Town there in the most convenient Place. The Lots to be 80 Feet front and 240 deep. The Number of Lots that shall be laid off at first will depend on the Number of Applications. The Purchase Money of each Lot to be four *Spanish* Dollars, and one Dollar per Annum Quitrent for ever. The Purchasers to build within the Space of two Years from the first of *December* next, on each Lot, a Log-House not less than sixteen Feet square, with a Stone or Brick Chimney; and as in that Country it will be necessary the first Settlers should build compactly, the Improvements must naturally join each other. It is farther proposed, for the Convenience of the Settlers, that an out Lot of ten Acres, contiguous to the Town, shall be laid off, for such as desire the same, at an easy Rent, on a long Lease. Attendance will be given by the Patentees at *Pittsburg*, till the Middle of *June*, at which Time one of them will set off from thence to execute the Plan. The advantageous Situation of that Place, formed by Nature as a temporary Magazine, or Repository, to receive the Produce of the very extensive and fertile Country on the *Ohio* and its Branches, as well as the necessary Merchandises suitable for the Inhabitants that shall emigrate into that Country (as Boats of fifty Tuns Burthen may be navigated from *New Orleans* up to the Town) is sufficient to recommend it; but when it is considered how liberal, nay profuse, Nature has been to it otherwise, in stocking it so abundantly that the slightest Industry may supply the most numerous Family with the greatest Plenty and amazing Variety of Fish, Fowl, and Flesh; the Fertility of the Soil, and Facility of Cultivation, that fit it for producing Commodities of great Value with little Labour; the Wholesomeness of the Waters, and Serenity of the Air, which render it healthy; and when Property may be so easily acquired, we may, with Certainty, affirm that it will in a short Time be equalled by few inland Places on the AMERICAN Continent.

(II)   JOHN CAMPBELL.
                        JOHN CONNOLLY.

Dunmore's War postponed first settlement planned at the Falls.

4.

After training his troops at the Falls in 1778, George Rogers Clark secured the Illinois country for America. In Feb. 1779, he led 170 men across flooded plains to capture Henry Hamilton and the British-held Fort Sackville at Vincennes.

5.

G. R. Clark was Kentucky's first military and civil leader and Louisville's founder.

6.

Harassed by pro-British Indians, frontiersmen called Lt. Gov. Henry Hamilton of Detroit the "hair buyer."

7.

14.

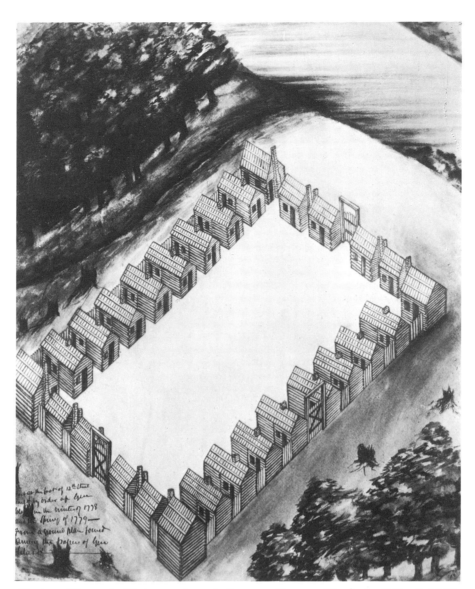

Fort-on-Shore built by order of George Rogers Clark in fall of 1778.

8.

Water fountain at Twelfth and Rowan marked fort's location in 1912.

9.

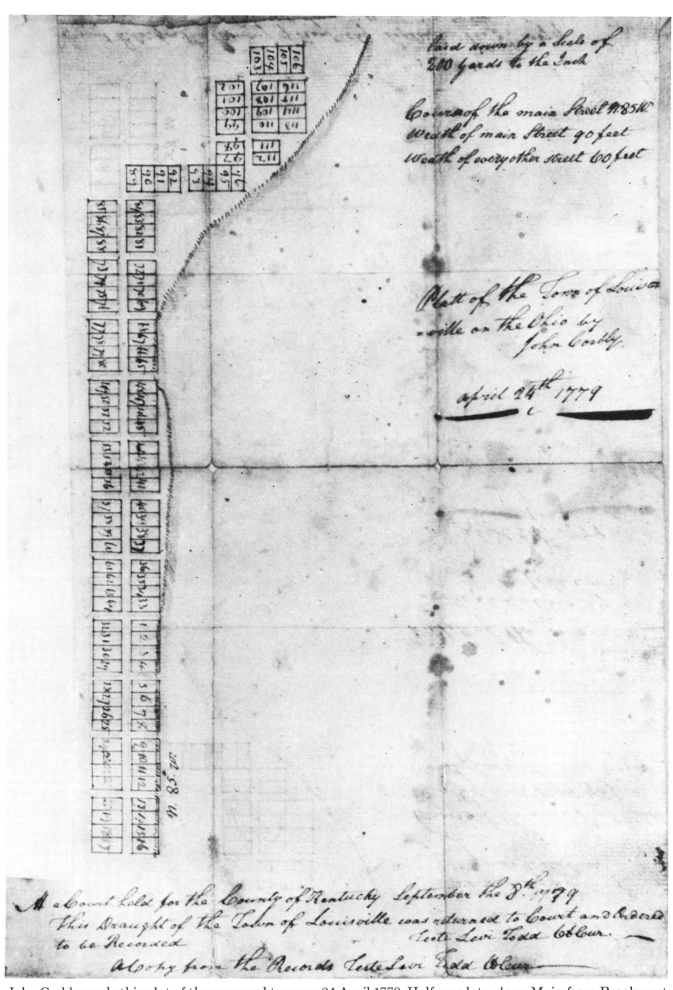

15.

John Corbly made this plat of the proposed town on 24 April 1779. Half-acre lots along Main from Brook past Thirteenth were given to settlers willing to cultivate land and build a 16′x20′ log house by Christmas.

10.

16.

In May 1780, the Virginia Legislature officially established Louisville, named for King Louis XVI who supported America in the Revolution.

11.

Thomas Jefferson was governor when the Virginia Legislature divided Kentucky County in 1780. Bronze statue of Jefferson, executed by Moses Ezekiel in 1899, is shown in front of the Courthouse in 1906. Work was a gift of the Bernheim family.

12.

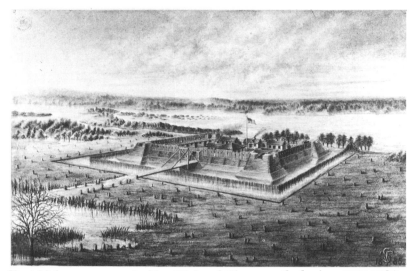

Fort Nelson was erected by Richard Chenoweth during 1781-1782.

13.

Site of Fort Nelson at 7th and Main near the old Union Depot.

14.

There are several good log houses building here, but the extravagance in wages, and laziness of the tradesmen keep back the improvement of the place exceedingly — in truth I see very little doing but card-playing, drinking and other vices among the common people, and am sorry too many of the better sort are too much engaged in the same manner, a few storekeepers excepted, who seem busy in land and other speculations, in which the veracity or generosity of some are not very conspicuous, being ever on the watch to take the advantage of the ignorance or innocence of the stranger . . . I find on the lower part of the falls the greatest abundance of swans, geese, ducks, and pigeons very plenty flying over, here are also fine fish, but the people [are] generally too indolent to catch them, though in great need.

Richard Butler, 1786.

As Louisville's log residences, taverns and shops built along the river front probably appeared from Clarksville in the 1780's.

15.

18.

Falls of Ohio.

PROPOSALS for laying off a Town at the Lower Falls, adjoining to Campbell's ware-house, on the lands of John Campbell.

1st. THAT 48 acres of land on the second bank be laid off into streets and ninety-six lots:

2d. The principal or main street to be at least 80 feet wide, and all others 60 ; the whole to be laid out into 6 squares of 16 lots in each square ; the front to be two such squares, and the other four to be laid off back of those.

3d. That the irregularities of the bank may not incommode the street, the front (that is the main) street, will be laid off at least 30 feet clear of them, and no lots to be laid off on the north side of that street at present.

4th. That every purchaser of a lot be obliged to build a dwelling-house of 16 feet square, at least, with a brick or stone chimney, in two years after he becomes a purchaser ; if he does not, then the said John Campbell shall be at liberty to dispose of the lot belonging to the said defaulter, to any other person who is willing to become a purchaser.

5th. So soon as the town is laid out, which I expect will be in March next, I will treat with any person who is willing to become an inhabitant ; and whatever lots remain unsold, on the 2d day of August next, I will dispose of at public sale, in the said town, that day, subject to the above terms of improvement.

My reasons for subjecting the lots to improvement, is to encourage settlers and prevent monopoly and jobbing ; as soon therefore, as the town is laid off I will make known the terms, which I intend shall be generous.

Jan. 2d, 1784.   JOHN CAMPBELL.

N. B. The act of assembly for establishing the town of Louisville, above the falls, was suspended last May session, and repealed so far as it interfered with mine or my partner's property, the last session.

I have several tracts of land of the first quality on Chartier's creek, from 12 to 4 miles distant from Fort Pitt, and on Elk Horn, Hickman's and Brashier's creeks, in the Kentucky country, which I would sell. Enquire of Mr. Bernard Gratz, Philadelphia ; Mr. Alexander W. Davey, in Baltimore ; capt. Philip Ross, on Chartier's creek, or myself at the falls of Ohio, where I intend to be from the middle of March till the end of May next ; I shall be in Philadelphia the latter part of this month, and at Pittsburgh from the middle to the end of February.

I can serve any gentleman possessed of officers or soldiers rights to lands in the state of Virginia, who wants to lay them to advantage, by recommending a person who will do it on the share.

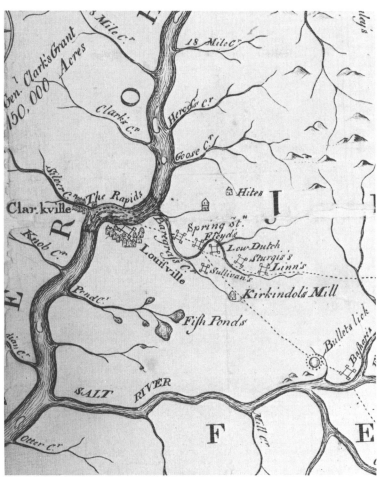

Section of first map of Kentucky published by Filson in 1784.

17.

19.

Signed sketch of cartographer and historian John Filson.

18.

Adjoining springhouses are all that remain of early stations. Group was probably examining A'Sturgus' station near Oxmoor in 1923.
19.

Surveyor John Floyd built two stations in 1779, one near this springhouse off Breckinridge Lane. He was ambushed by Indians in 1783.
20.

Cato Watts is remembered as a fine fiddle player and the first criminal hanged in Louisville. Court records do not confirm Cato's execution for killing his owner John Donne
in 1786, but they do list several others who would have preceded him to the gallows.

22.

View of Louisville from near Clarksville

Engrav'd & Printed by John Goodmon Frankfort Kentucky 1806

Inset from 1806 map of the Falls area by Jared Brooks shows earliest view of Louisville's river front and County Courthouse at right.
22.

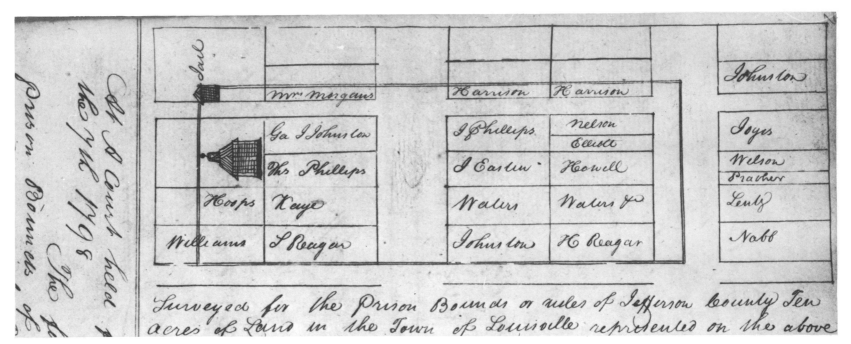

Surveyed for the Prison Bounds or rules of Jefferson County Ten acres of Land in the Town of Louisville represented on the above

Outlines of Courthouse and Jail appear on 1798 prison bounds plan. Jail trustees were permitted to walk within the ten acre bounds.
23.

Louis Ville is the County Town of Jefferson is situated immediately on Banks of Ohio. the situation is beautiful and I think this place may in time be of Consequence altho its now an inconsiderable V[i]llage. Louis Ville has about 30 Houses but there is not an Elegant Hous in the place. the Court Hous is of Stone and built with some Taste. at this place I see a Number of Indians from the Nations over the Ohio, Piankishas Delawares and Wyatenas. Notwithstanding Louis Ville is the landing place of all Boats that Come Down the Ohio and Bound to any place below the Falls in consequence of which there is a great resort of Companey yit there is Not a Tavern in the place that deserves a better name than that of Grog Shop. Louis Ville by nature is beautifull but the handy work of Man has insted of improving destroy.d the works of Nature and made it a detestable place.

Moses Austin, 1797.

In 1789, General G. R. Clark retired to his father's Mulberry Hill tract off Poplar Level Road to write about his military exploits.

24.

The Ballards and Mortons, collateral descendants of General Clark, are about to return home after an outing to Mulberry Hill in 1907.

25.

24.

Remnants of frontier log construction show "dog trot" was later enclosed and plastered to make entrance hall. Note sign of stair.

26.

Outbuildings clustered around remains of the 1785 log house at right were removed during World War I to make way for Camp Taylor.

27.

Cartoon depicts practice continued from the Revolution to the War of 1812.

28.

Father took most pride in a stone spring-house which he built on the side of the branch about two hundred yards from the house . . . [he] meant this to be used as a kind of fort, as well as a spring-house. . . . On July 17th all the white folks after supper were lingering around the table when suddenly the outside door opened and a party of sixteen Indians, yelling with their utmost fury, burst into the room. . . . we all ran in every direction, and mother had started toward the spring-house, when she was shot between the shoulder blades with an arrow. . . . The Indian followed her, and . . . then began his triumphant work of scalping her. . . . She suffered from her wounds for a long time but finally fully recovered. However, she was a curiosity to see — without hair, or any place on her head for it to grow.

James Chenoweth, [1789]

25.

Chenoweth springhouse off Avoca Road near Middletown is site of massacre.

29.

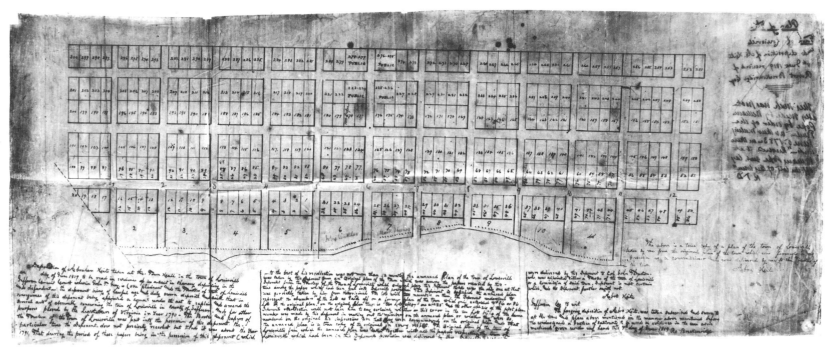

26. In 1791 Abraham Hite copied the "original plan" of Louisville, probably prepared by William Pope in 1783. Lots extended to Liberty St.

30.

Engraved for Imlay's American Topography.

CLARKVILLE

From A to B a Canal
is intended to be cut.

The Dotted Line marks
the Channel of the River.

Scale of Yards.

LOUISVILLE

Published Feb'y 1795 by J. Debrett, Piccadilly, London.

Imlay's *American Topography* (London, 1793) updated earlier maps wit

View of the Falls and Louisville made from Clarksville during Victor Collot's 1796 expedition.

31.

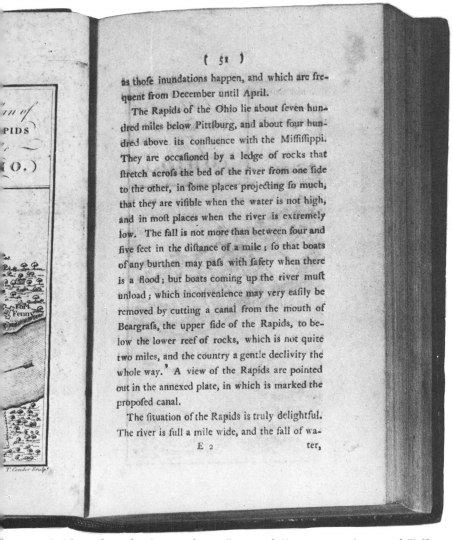

as those inundations happen, and which are frequent from December until April.

The Rapids of the Ohio lie about seven hundred miles below Pittsburg, and about four hundred above its confluence with the Mississippi. They are occasioned by a ledge of rocks that stretch across the bed of the river from one side to the other, in some places projecting so much, that they are visible when the water is not high, and in most places when the river is extremely low. The fall is not more than between four and five feet in the distance of a mile; so that boats of any burthen may pass with safety when there is a flood; but boats coming up the river must unload; which inconvenience may very easily be removed by cutting a canal from the mouth of Beargrass, the upper side of the Rapids, to below the lower reef of rocks, which is not quite two miles, and the country a gentle declivity the whole way. A view of the Rapids are pointed out in the annexed plate, in which is marked the proposed canal.

The situation of the Rapids is truly delightful. The river is full a mile wide, and the fall of wa-

E 2   ter,

houses, fields and garden lots and was first to delineate canal around Falls.

32.

27.

28.

William Clark and nine other Kentuckians met Meriwether Lewis at Louisville and departed the Falls *on a Western Tour*, 26 Oct. 1803.

33.

Bush's *ca.* 1817 portrait of Genl. William Clark, whose elder brother George Rogers Clark had been asked to lead a Pacific expedition by Jefferson in 1783.

34.

LOUISVILLE, October 15.
Captain Lewis arrived at this port on Friday laſt. We are informed, that he has brought barges &c. on a new conſtruction, that can be taken in pieces, for the purpoſe of paſſing carrying-places ; and that he and captain Clark will ſtart in a few days on their expedition to the Weſtward.

35.

LOUISVILLE, October 29.
Capt Clark and Mr. Lewis left this place on Wedneſday laſt, on the expedition to the Weſtward. We have not been enabled to aſcertain what length this rout will extend, as when it was firſt ſet on foot by the Preſident, the Louiſiana country was not ceded to the United States, and it is likely it will be conſiderably extended—they are to receive further inſtructions at Kahokia. It is, however, certain that they will aſcend the main branch of the Miſſiſſippi, as far as poſſible : and it is probable they will then direct their courſe to the Miſſouri, and aſcend it. They have the iron frame of a boat, intended to be covered with ſkins, which can, by ſcrews, be formed into one or four, as may beſt ſuit their purpoſes. About 60 men will compoſe the party.

36.

30.

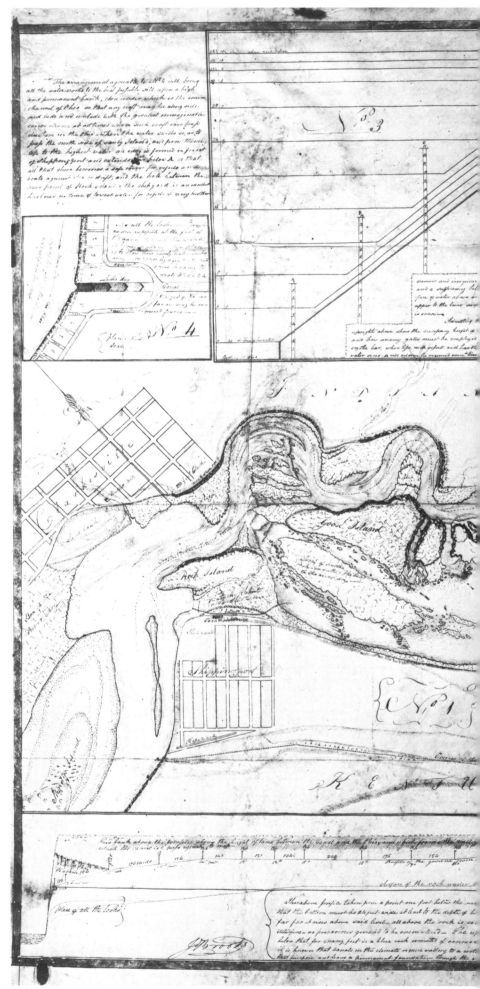

Jared Brooks' detailed, *circa* 1805 map shows two ships wrecked in rapic

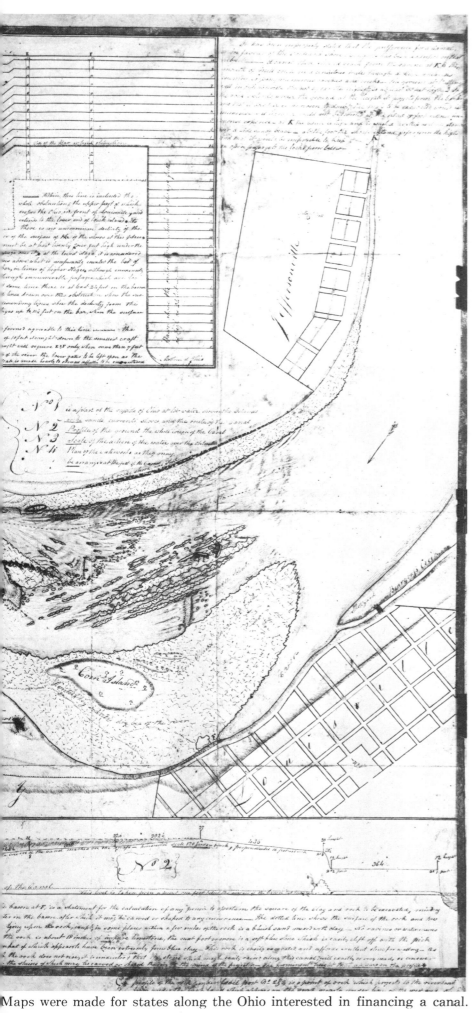

Maps were made for states along the Ohio interested in financing a canal.

32.

38.

Audubon painted Hooded Mergansers and Cardinal at the Falls.

39.

Now extinct, Passenger Pigeons were abundant at the Falls when naturalist John James Audubon operated a general store in Louisville between 1808-1810.

40.

Audubon once estimated 9,000 Swallows roosted in large sycamore near Louisville.

41.

Beargrass Creek . . . The spot on which I witnessed the celebration of an anniversary of the glorious proclamation of our independence is situated on its banks near the city of Louisville . . . Each denizen had freely given his ox, his ham, his venison, his Turkeys and other fowls. Here were to be seen flagons of every beverage used in the country; "la belle riviere" had opened her finny stores, the melons of all sorts, peaches, plums, and pears, would have sufficed to stock a market . . . Columns of smoke from newly kindled fires rose above the trees; fifty cooks or more moved to and fro as they plied their trade; waiters of all qualities were disposing the dishes, the glasses and the punch-bowls, amid vases filled with rich wines. "Old Monongahela" filled many a barrel for the crowd . . . In a short time the ground was alive with merriment. A great wooden cannon bound with iron hoops was now crammed with home-made powder; fire was conveyed to it by means of a train, and as the explosion burst forth, thousands of hearty huzzas mingled with its echoes. From the most learned a good oration fell in proud and gladdening words on every ear . . . Fifes and drums sounded the march which had ever led him [Washington] to glory; and as they changed to our celebrated "Yankee-Doodle," the air again rang with acclamations . . . You would have been pleased to see those who did not join in the dance shooting at distant marks with their heavy rifles, or watched how they showed off the superior speed of their high bred "Old Virginia" horses . . .

John James Audubon, [*ca.* 1809]

Shippingport merchant James Berthoud was helpful to Audubon.

42.

Audubon sketched the Berthouds about 1820. Son Nicholas became his manager.

43.

Tarascon mills at Shippingport during 1883 flood. In 1958, residents abandoned the frequently inundated island created by the canal.
44.

34.

McHarry Hotel was named for Tarascon mill superintendant.
45.

Old Tarascon flour mill prior to its destruction by fire in 1892.
46.

A ship yard is erected below the rapids, by the company of Tavascon [Tarascon] Brothers, and James Berthand [Berthoud], the latter of whom now resides here. This certainly is the most eligible place on the river Ohio; and a greater prospect of the advantages of such an establishment now opens, since the vast territory of Louisiana has become the property of the United States.

Louisville is a port of entry. It is about nine hundred and thirteen miles by way of the river and mountains to Philadelphia, and by land about seven hundred. It is seventy miles from Lexington, and forty from Frankfort, in Kentucky, of which State it forms a part, and conducts all its export, which principally consists of the articles before named, and which are taken in exchange for foreign spirits and British goods, brought into the country by the way of Pittsburg.

The inhabitants are universally addicted to gambling and drinking. The billiard rooms are crowded from morning to night, and often all night through. I am the more concerned to see the prevalence of these vices, as I experience a liberality and attention in the town, which has given me an interest in the general welfare of its people.

Thomas Ashe, 1806.

The population of Shippingport, may be estimated at 600 souls, including strangers. Some taste is already perceptible in the construction of their houses, many of which are neatly built and ornamented with galleries, in which, of a Sunday, are displayed all the beauty of the place. It is, in fact, the "Bois de Bouloigne" of Louisville, it being the resort of all classes, on high days and holidays.

At these times, it exhibits a spectacle at once novel and interesting. The number of steam boats in the port, each bearing one or two flags, the throng of horses, carriages, and gigs, and the contented appearance of a crowd of pedestrians, all arrayed in their "Sunday's best," produce an effect it would be impossible to describe.

There were formerly here, as at Louisville, a number of rope walks, which are at present nearly all abandoned, there not being a sufficiency of hemp raised in the county to supply the manufacturers. This has arisen from the great losses sustained in the sales of cordage, which has discouraged the rope maker, and, consequently, offered no inducement to the farmer, to plant an article for which there was but little demand . . .

Merchant Manufacturing Mill. This valuable mill is remarkable, not only for its size and the quantity of flour it is calculated to manufacture when completed, but for the beauty of its machinery, which is said to be the most perfect specimen of the millwright's abilities to be found in this or any other country. The foundations were commenced in June, 1815, and were ready to receive the enormous superstructure only in the spring of 1817. The building is divided into six stories, considerably higher than is usual, there being 102 feet from the first to the sixth.

Henry McMurtrie, 1819

Spring Station on Trinity Road is an early example of Federal style. It was started by Samuel Beal in 1795 on the site of a pioneer log fort.

47.

Ridgeway off Massie Ave., prior to restoration. Built *circa* 1805, it is one of the nation's finest examples of Federal domestic architecture.

48.

36.

1899 view of home Gwathmey built *ca.* 1810 on Sixth near Cedar.
49.

John Gwathmey built the Indian Queen Hotel about 1803 and operated it until 1819 when he sold out and left town. He also had just built the third courthouse.
50.

Louisville is said to be improving in health: the prevalent diseases are fever and ague; besides which, the common disorders of this State are consumption, pleurisy, typhus, remittent and intermittent fevers, rheumatism, and dysentery. I do not feel myself competent to confirm or deny the general claim of the Kentuckians to generosity and warmth of character; of their habits I would wish to speak with equal diffidence; that they drink a great deal, swear a great deal, and gamble a great deal, will be apparent to a very brief resident . . .

Having been twice at Louisville, I boarded at both the hotels (Allen's, Washington Hall, and Gwathing's [Gwathmey's], Indian Queen): they are similar establishments, both upon a very large scale, the former having an average of 80 boarders per day, the latter of 140 . . . A person desiring to put up at one of them, applies to the bar-keeper, and he must not feel disappointed should he be refused admittance from want of room. The place for washing is in the open yard, in which there is a large cistern, several towels, and a negro in attendance. The sleeping-room commonly contains from 4 to 8 bed-steads, having mattresses, but frequently no feather-beds; sheets of calico, two blankets, a quilt (either a cotton counterpane, or made of patchwork); the bedsteads have no curtains, and the rooms are generally unprovided with any conveniences. The public rooms are a news-room, a boot-room, in which the bar is situated, and a dining-room. The fires are generally surrounded by parties of about six, who gain and keep possession. The usual custom is to pace up and down the news-room in a manner similar to walking the deck at sea. Smoking segars is practised by all without an exception, and at every hour of the day. Argument or discussion in this part of the world is of very rare occurence; social intercourse seems still more unusual; conversation on general topics, or the taking enlarged and enlightened views of things, rarely occurs; each man is in pursuit of his own individual interest, and follows it in an individualized manner. But to return to the taverns: at half past seven, the first bell rings for the purpose of collecting all the boarders, and at eight the second bell rings; breakfast is then set, the dining-room is unlocked, a general rush commences, and some activity, as well as dexterity, is essentially necessary to obtain a seat at the table. A boy, as clerk, attends to take down the names, in order that when bills are settled no improper deduction should be made. The breakfast consists of a profuse supply of fish, flesh, and fowl, which is consumed with a rapidity truly extraordinary; often before I had finished my first cup of tea, the room, which when I had commenced was crowded to suffocation, had become nearly empty.

At half-past one, the first bell rings, announcing the approach of dinner; the avenues to the dining-room become thronged. At two o'clock the second bell rings, the doors are thrown open, and a repetition of the breakfast scene succeeds. At six, tea, or what is here called supper, is announced, and partaken of in the same manner. This is the last meal, and usually affords the same fare as breakfast. A billiard table adjoins the hotel, and is generally well occupied. At ten o'clock, nearly all have gone to bed, or what they call "turned in." At table there is neither conversation nor yet drinking; the latter is effected by individuals taking their solitary "eye openers," "toddy," and "phlegm dispersers," at the bar, the keeper of which is in full employ from sun-rise to bedtime. A large tub of water, with a ladle, is placed on the bar, to which customers go and help themselves. When spirits are called for, the decanter is handed, and you take what quantity you please; the charge is always 6-3/4d. It is never drunk neat, or with sugar or warm water. The life of boarders at an American tavern, presents the most senseless and comfortless mode of killing time which I have ever seen. Every house of this description that I have been in is thronged to excess, and there is not a man who appears to have a single earthly object in view, except spitting and smoking segars. I have not seen a book in the hands of any person since I left Philadelphia. Objectionable as these habits are, they afford decided evidence of the prosperity of that country, which can admit so large a body of its citizens to waste in indolence three-fourths of their lives, and would also appear to hold out encouragement to Englishmen with English habits, who could retain their industry amid a nation of indolence, and have sufficient firmness to live in America, and yet bid defiance to the deadly example of its natives.

Henry Bradshaw Fearon, 1817.

Patten family lot in Western Cemetery at 16th and Jefferson. Louisville's second graveyard replaced smaller one at 11th and Jefferson.

51.

James Patten, pioneer, Indian fighter and Falls pilot.

53.

Patten family was one of original six to settle at Falls.

52.

38.

City trustees reserved four lots south of Jefferson between 11th and 12th as a public burying ground in 1786. It was closed in 1832.

54.

In 1880, Mayor John Baxter converted the derelict cemetery into a park which was destroyed by the 1890 tornado. It was later rebuilt.

55.

39.

Joseph H. Bush painted a forlorn Gen. George Rogers Clark shortly before *the Father of the West* died at Locust Grove in 1818.

40.

George Rogers Clark lived with his sister Lucy Clark Croghan and her family at Locust Grove from 1809 until his death in 1818.

57.

Lucy's husband, Major William Croghan, was Clark's deputy surveyor, a town trustee and a speculator in land and trade.

58.

Back of Locust Grove on Blankenbaker Lane prior to purchase and restoration by Commonwealth and County. Built about 1790 by Croghan on a 793 acre tract, it entertained as guests: Audubon, Burr, Lewis and Clark, Cassius Clay, Monroe, Jackson and Taylor.

59.

Locust Grove's front elevation in juxtaposed photographs before (right) and after (left) restoration. Historic Homes Foundation has operated museum since 1964 as a memorial to General Clark.

60.

An invalid, General Clark resided in this downstairs bedroom. He was buried at Locust Grove, but later reinterred in Cave Hill Cemetery. Walnut paneling is a notable feature of the restoration.

61.

42.

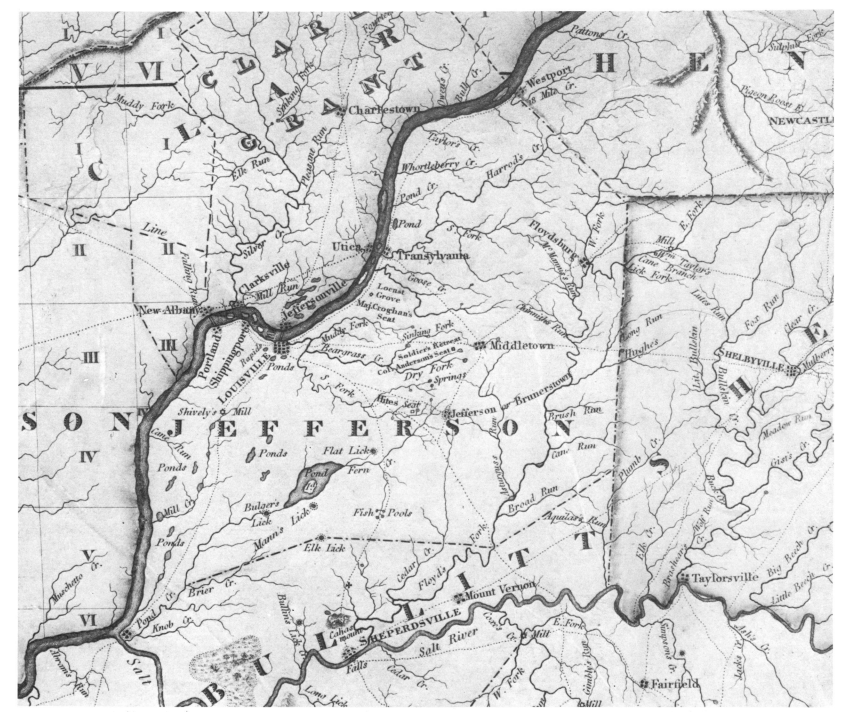

A section from the finely delineated 1819 map of Kentucky and the Northwest Territory published by the surveyor Luke Munsell.

62.

In the early days of the town, there were many large ponds of water in almost every direction, some of which were very useful to the early settler, as affording a sufficient supply of water for manufacturing purposes, and served also for washing, it being a difficult task to obtain water from the river, in sufficient quantities, in consequence of a deep ravine which made the road to the landing circuitous, and often almost impassable . . .

There are some amusing reminiscences of Grayson's Pond. We have it from a citizen, who well remembers the outlines of this pond. Great numbers of tortoise or small turtle, were found about this pond. Thither, also, came to enjoy its luxuries, large flocks of geese and ducks. The battles between these different tribes are described as being very amusing. The turtle would take to the water and skull along very silently, and settling beneath the surface, await the approach of the duck; at a sudden, he would seize the duck by his feet and draw him under water. The struggle generally resulted in favor of the feathered combatant, who, on regaining the surface would set up such shouts as to collect the whole flock around him an a grand congratulatory quacking convention.

This pond, well shaded by the native forest trees, became a favorite resort of many, to while away the hours of a sultry day on its banks. It was always clear, and had a sufficient depth of water, the dryest season to swim a horse in.

Another pond, at this period, (1800) and a very disagreeable one, was to be met with at the intersection of 3rd and Market streets, extending along Third street to nearly opposite the site of the present post office. A Tannery on Third street, which discharged its wastewater into this pond, rendered it, at times, nearly impassable, except by mounting a rail-fence, which enclosed the lot where the White Mansion now stands. The wagons from the country often stalled at this point.

1844-45 Louisville Directory

Outbuildings off Hurstbourne Lane are all that remain of Soldier's Retreat, the *circa* 1790 home of Col. Richard C. Anderson.

63.

In 1910, the Kaetin family lived on the tract visited by Pres. James Monroe and Andrew Jackson in 1819 and Lafayette in 1825.

64.

44.

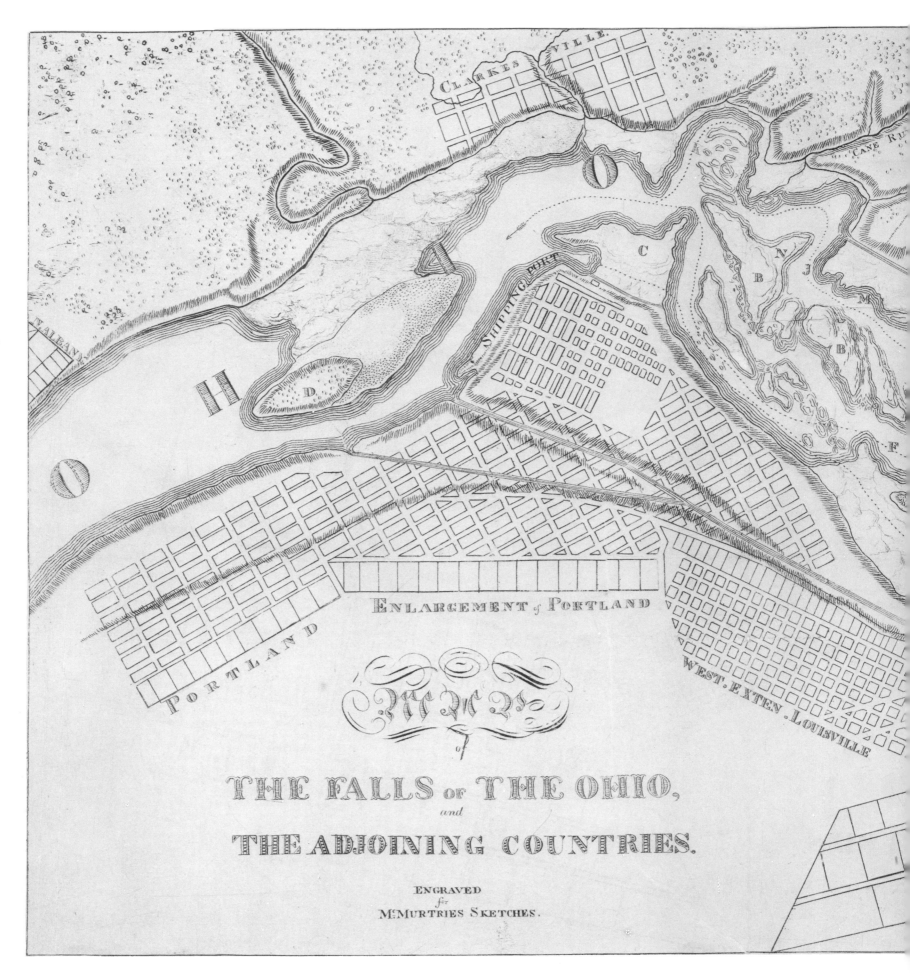

MAP
of
THE FALLS OF THE OHIO,
and
THE ADJOINING COUNTRIES.

ENGRAVED
for
McMURTRIES SKETCHES.

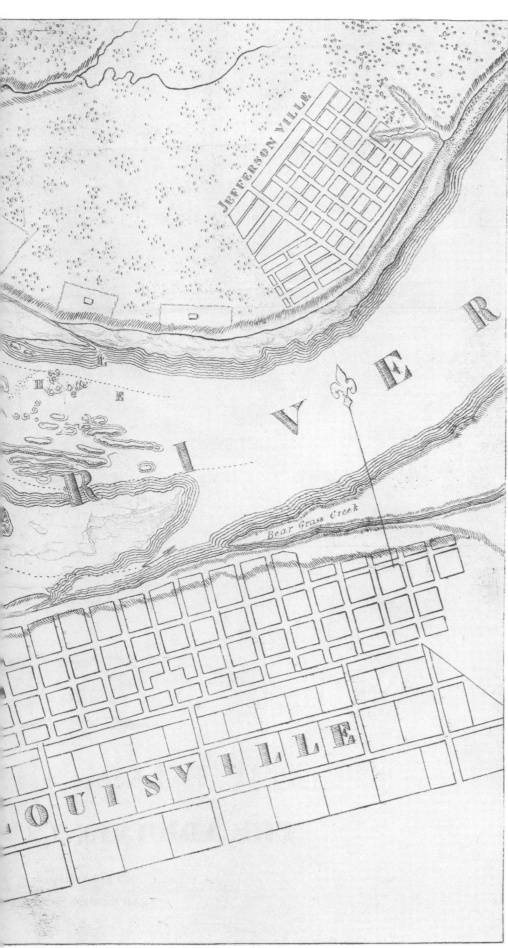

65.

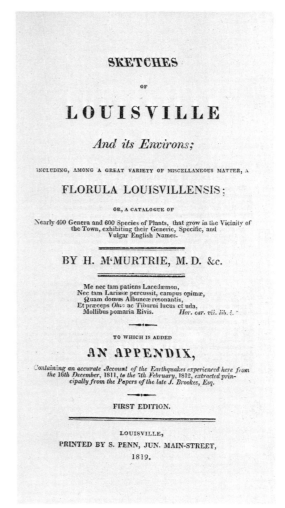

66.

45.

Henry McMurtrie wrote city's first history.

67.

46.

Blue Staffordshire plate by Enoch Wood & Sons *ca.* 1825 shows Louisville Marine Hospital.
68.

Dr. Ferguson, a physician here, carried us to the hospital. This edifice lies insulated upon a small eminence. The building was commenced several years ago, and is not yet finished. The state of Kentucky gave the ground as a donation, and bears a part of the expenses of building. As the establishment is principally used for the reception of sick seamen, congress has given the hospital a revenue from the custom-house in New Orleans. The hospital consists of a basement story, three stories above, and wings, which each have a basement and two stories. In the basement of the centre building, are the kitchen, wash-house, the store-rooms, &c., and in the upper story, the chamber for the meeting of the directors, the apothecary's room, the steward's dwelling, and the state rooms for patients paying board and lodging. In the third story a theatre for surgical operations will be arranged. In the wings are roomy and well aired apartments for the white patients, and in the basement, those for the negroes and coloured persons. Slavery is still permitted in Kentucky. There has been until now only one apartment habitable, in which twelve patients are lying. These have cleanly beds, but only wooden bedsteads. When the building is thoroughly finished, it will contain at least one hundred and fifty persons with comfort. Such an establishment is extremely necessary for such a place as Louisville, which is very unhealthy in summer ...

Dr. Ferguson was very much occupied in vaccination. The natural small-pox had made its appearance within a few days, under a very malignant form, in the town. On this account every one had their children vaccinated as speedily as possible; even those who were prejudiced against vaccination.

Bernhard, Duke of Saxe-Weimar Eisenach, 1826.

Advent of steamboat traffic on Ohio enhanced Louisville's commerce and her problems too. Citizens burdened by caring for influx of homeless, sick and injured mariners in their homes, caused first hospital to be started in 1817.

69.

Admitting patients by 1823, Louisville Marine Hospital was supported originally by State funds and a 2% levy on auctions in Jefferson County. 1856 engraving shows removal of front ornamentation and addition of balconies to wings.

70.

48.

When control was given to City by the Commonwealth in 1826, name was changed to Louisville City Hospital. Old core and additions (above) were razed and replaced by present General Hospital in 1914.

71.

U.S. Marine Hospital built in 1847 is frequently confused with the Louisville Marine Hospital. One of about ten federal hospitals for boatmen, it later became the Louisville Memorial Hospital.

72.

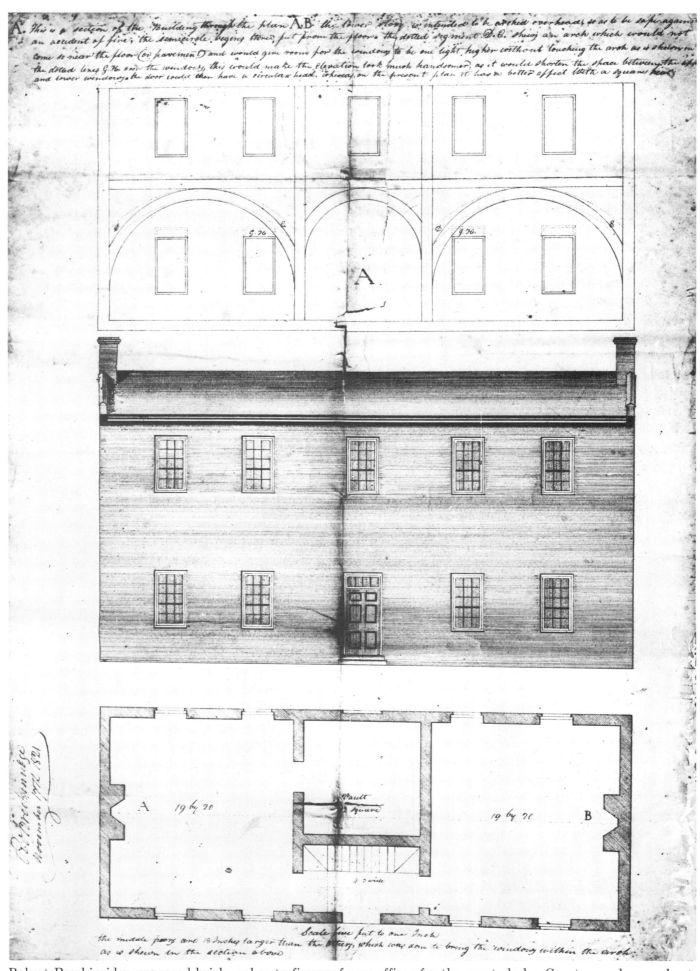

49.

Robert Breckinridge proposed brick arches to fireproof new offices for the court clerks. Court records were kept in this brick office on the northwest corner of 6th and Jefferson near the old courthouse from 1824 until 1842.

50.

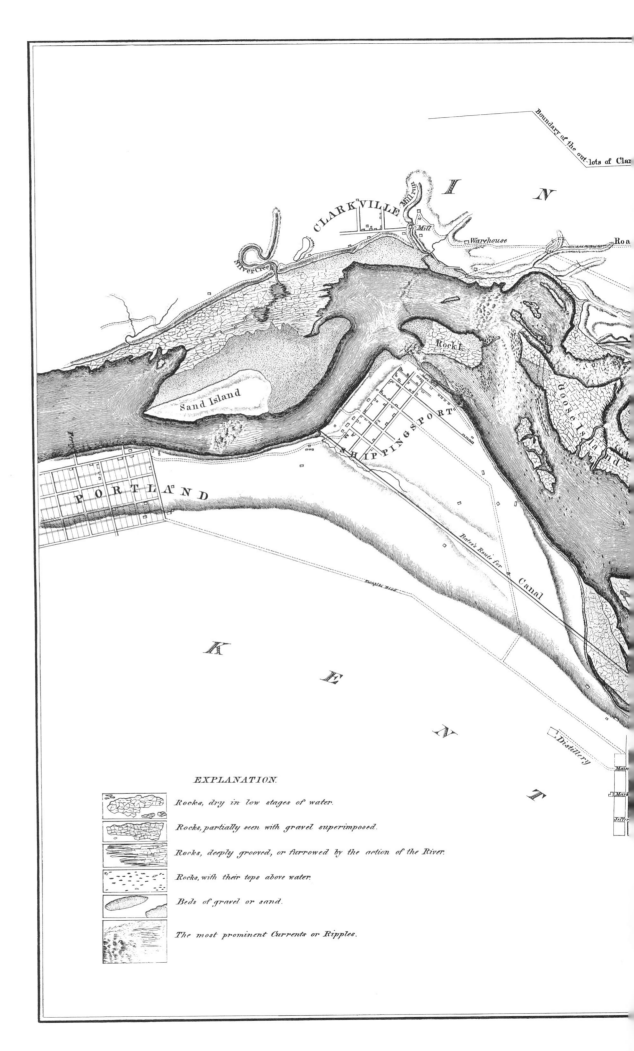

EXPLANATION.

Rocks, dry in low stages of water.

Rocks, partially seen with gravel superimposed.

Rocks, deeply grooved, or furrowed by the action of the River.

Rocks, with their tops above water.

Beds of gravel or sand.

The most prominent Currents or Ripples.

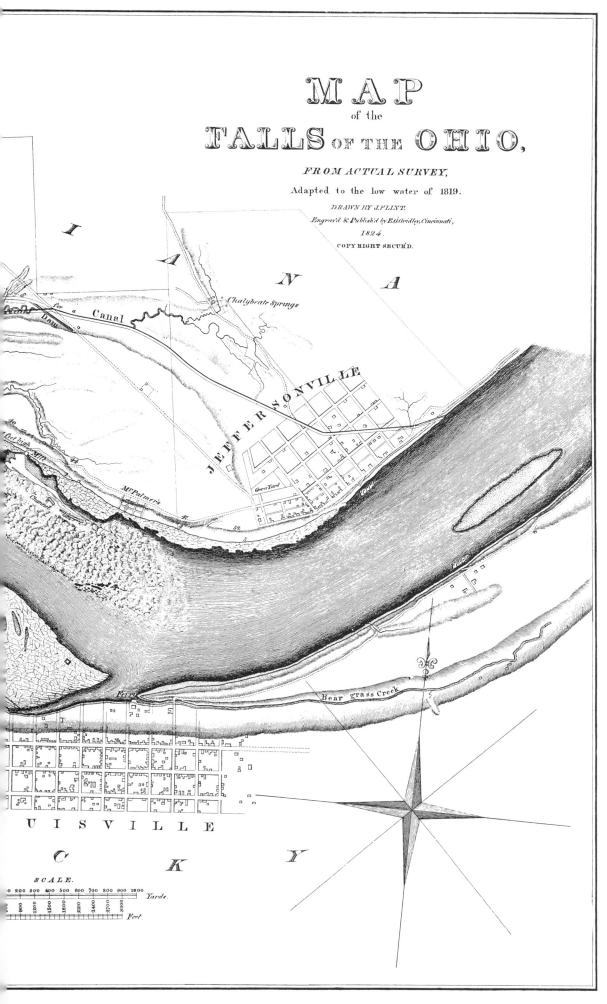

MAP
of the
FALLS OF THE OHIO,
FROM ACTUAL SURVEY,
Adapted to the low water of 1819.

DRAWN BY J. FLINT.

Engrav'd & Publish'd by E. Gitraidley, Cincinnati,
1824.

COPY RIGHT SECUR'D.

51.

SCALE.

0 200 300 400 500 600 700 800 900 1000   Yards.

Feet.

52.

Staffordshire dish attributed to J. & R. Clews pictures Louisville's waterfront about 1825. Mouth of Beargrass Creek is at left; 4th St. runs into the public wharf in center; and 5th St. is indicated at right.

75.

John B. H. Latrobe's 1833 watercolor of Gray's warehouse and wharf area near foot of 4th St. Slope of the public landing was completely paved for easy access of boats. Note similarity with scene on dish above.

76.

Christ Church built on 2nd north of Walnut in 1824-1825
was remembered to have had this appearance originally.

77.

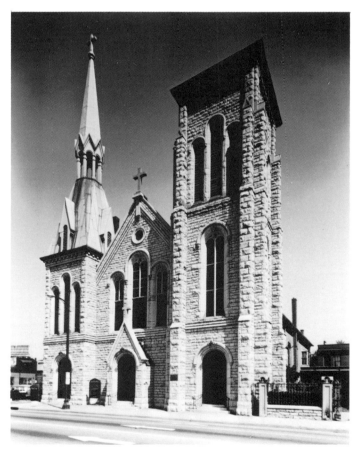

Facade of Louisville's first Episcopal Church altered
in 1872. Church was consecrated as a Cathedral in 1894.

78.

Sketch of steamboat *De Witt Clinton*. Goose Island in background was adajcent Six Mile Island before disappearing in 1937 flood.

79.

View of sunset over Louisville from Six Mile Island. Both sketches made by French naturalist Charles Alexandre Lesueur in 1826.

80.

54.

Baptists and Masons built this brick structure on the S.W. corner of 5th and Liberty between 1824-26. Baptist Church occupied two floors, Masonic Hall the third. Kentucky School of Medicine moved here in 1850 after Walnut Street Baptist Church was finished.

81.

Louisville has several churches, tolerably well built; a new one was began, but on rather too large a scale. The pious funds were exhausted; therefore a lodge of freemasons undertook the finishing of this grand house, and kept it for their own use. The canal is destined to light vessels over the Ohio, when they cannot pass the falls on account of low water, and are obliged to discharge their cargo. It is apprehended however, that the money invested in the canal will not yield a great interest, as the time of service, for which the canal is required does not extend beyond three months. During six months of the year the Ohio is so low, that not a solitary boat can navigate it, and when it rises, it becomes so high, that the rocks which produce the rapids are covered, so that vessels can go up and down without danger. The labour on the canal has been commenced about six weeks. The banks in the neighbourhood of the canal are high, and present a beautiful prospect over the rapids, and the adjacent region, which is well cultivated and bounded by woody hills.

Bernhard, Duke of Saxe-Weimar Eisenach, 1826.

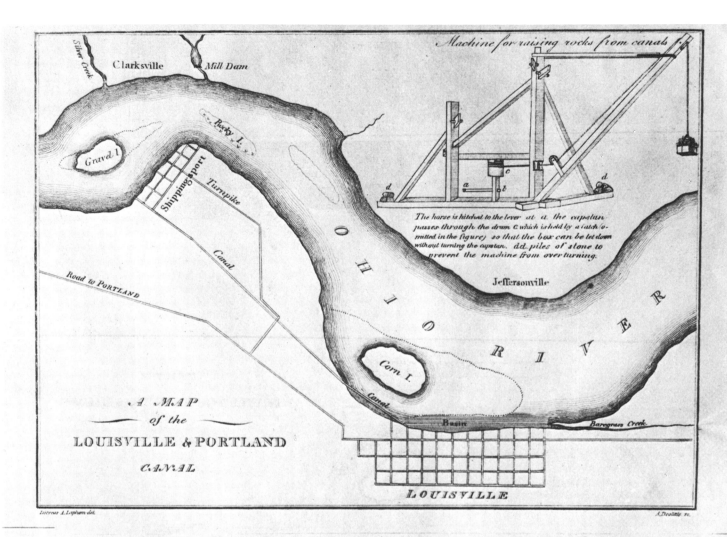

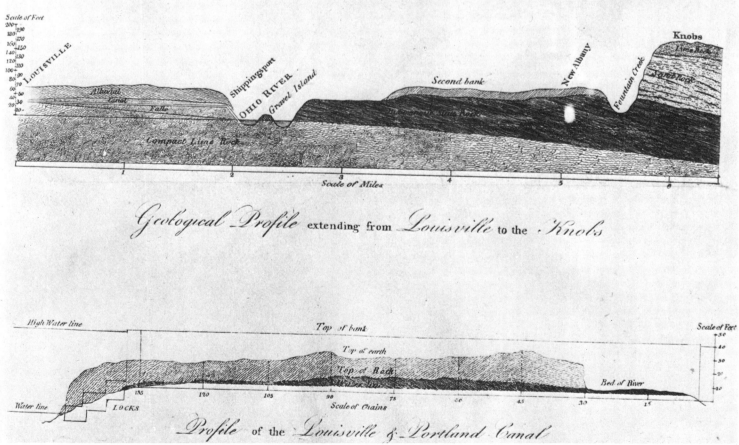

Sixteen year old Increase Lapham prepared illustrations for Silliman's *American Journal of Science and Arts* in 1828. While a rodman on the canal, Lapham made many scientific observations and managed to attend Mann Butler's school.

56.

View of the Ohio from Shippingport near Louisville in Kentucky. looking down the River. 14th May 1828

View of Ohio River and part of Shippingport, looking west probably from near the Tarascon mill site. Writer and traveler, Capt. Basil Hall, formerly of the British Navy, made at least four sketches of Louisville scenes with the camera lucida in May 1828.

83.

Study in a Forest of Kentucky near Louisville 10th May 1828

Hall wrote in his *Travels in North America,* "The trees, also, round Louisville were incomparably finer than any we had seen elsewhere, especially the sycamores. They were not only taller, but, having plenty of space...had grown up with singular beauty..."

84.

Hall noted this large sycamore with a nine foot diameter near Louisville in 1828.

85.

Hall sketched this rare example of Georgian architecture in Kentucky. John W. Hundley's home off Bardstown Road had a hipped roof and balustraded roof-deck. A devout Presbyterian, Hundley also built the original Beulah Church on this almost 1,200 acre tract.

86.

58.

Along every free flowing stream, water was harnessed to do work by a large water wheel connected to a drive shaft. Water mills provided power to grind flour, saw lumber and squeeze oil. This grist mill, off Wolf Pen Branch Road, was probably built in the 1820's.

Built for $750,000, Louisville and Portland Canal was opened in 1830 by the *Uncas*.
88.

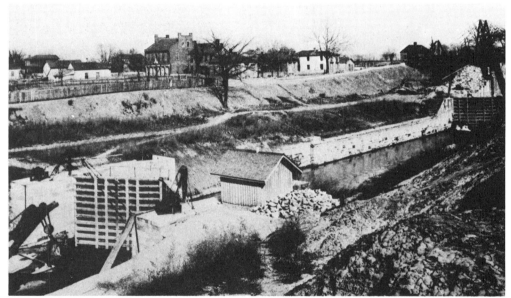

This view was made in 1872 when this obsolete lock system was being replaced.
89.

Before improvements, canal was two miles long, only 50 feet wide with four locks.
90.

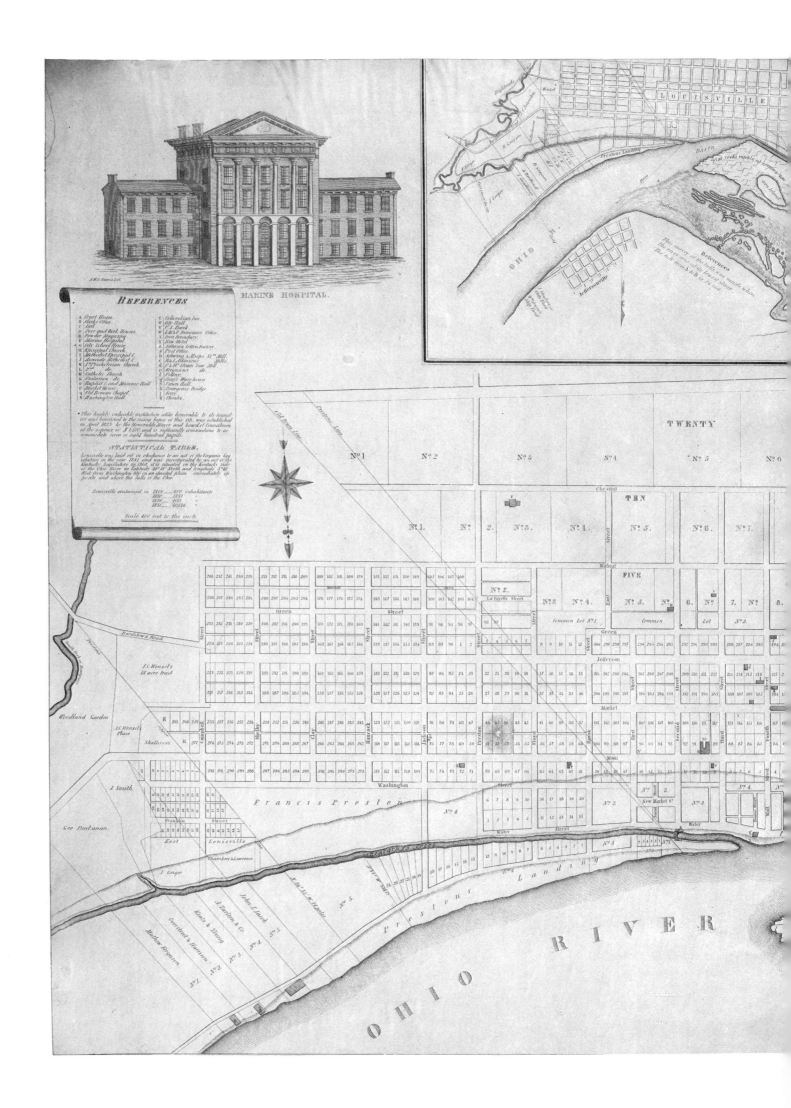

MARINE HOSPITAL.

REFERENCES

Scale 400 feet to the inch

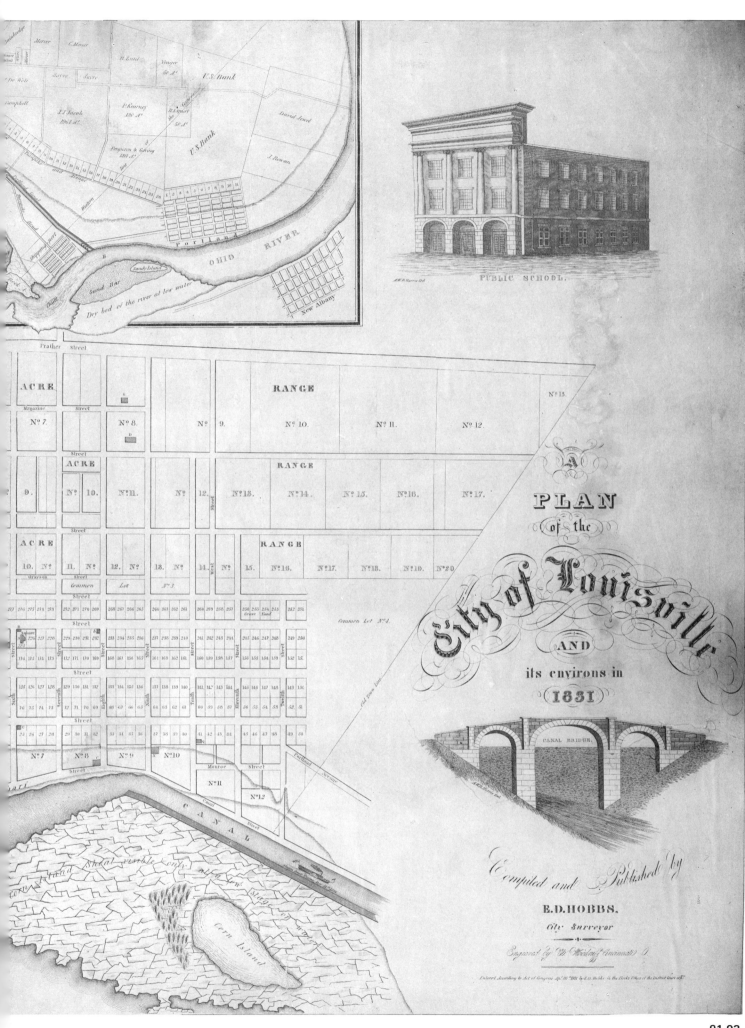

PUBLIC SCHOOL.

Prather street

ACRE

RANGE

Nº 13.

Nº 7.

Nº 8.

Nº 9.

Nº 10.

Nº 11.

Nº 12.

ACRE

RANGE

9.

Nº 10.

Nº 11.

Nº 12.

Nº 13.

Nº 14.

Nº 15.

Nº 16.

Nº 17.

ACRE

RANGE

10. Nº 11. Nº 12. Nº 13. Nº 14. West Nº 15. Nº 16. Nº 17. Nº 18. Nº 19. Nº 20.

PLAN
of the
City of Louisville
AND
its environs in
1831

CANAL BRIDGE

Compiled and Published by
E. D. HOBBS.
City Surveyor

Engraved by W. Woodruff, Cincinnati. O.

61.

CANAL

Corn Island

OHIO RIVER

Portland

New Albany

Sand Bar

Dry bed of the river at low water

U. S. Bank

BUILDING A HERITAGE 1830-1860

The old Bell tavern stood on the south side of Jefferson street, blocking up Sixth street. The court-house was then standing on the jail lot and fronting Sixth street, and the poverty row of that day was scattered along Sixth and along Jefferson streets.

Have you forgotten poor old Jake Martin and his dingy little bakery and grocery in the frame shanty on the south side of Main, between Fifth and Sixth, and Schafer's candy shop, with his candy marble jars, arranged in mosaics? There we candied and sodaed near enough to Shade's drug store to prevent damage from excess. We shod hard by at Mullikin's or at Beyroth's, and bought our spelling-books at Rice's book-store, adjoining. People in those days, who wanted a choice steak, had to be by daylight at the market-house, between Fourth and Fifth, with the mayor's office over it.

What an event it was when the old Harrison House on the corner of Main and Sixth streets and the house below were torn down to give way to those monstrous structures — the Franklin House, the Light House, and the Louisville Hotel of those days. How grand those new edifices looked to us as story was piled on story until we were lost in bewilderment at their immensity. We would not believe that Paris or London could boast of such colossal buildings. Nothing had equaled them since the days of the Temple or the Tower of Babel. I remember of telling a boy cousin that "Louisville had two houses bigger than his whole town."

What a wonderful place to us was the old theater on Jefferson, between Third and Fourth streets . . . Stickney's circus, before the circus had any of its new classic names, used to hold forth back of Scott Glore's present stand, and with the other boys you and I used to follow Lon Lipman and Frank Wilmot around the streets as though they were walking demigods, deeming it an honor if they would call us by name in the crowd. The elephant was the only lion, greater than a real acting circus boy. Excuse the bull. Ricards, you remember, was the clown. How racy and original were his jokes, the same that our grandfathers heard, the same that our grandchildren will laugh at. . . .

All below Twelfth street was a "waste," if not a howling wilderness. We had to drive up our cows from that "ilk," and you recollect what our boyish ideas were of the dangers of that part of the world if we were caught out alone by the dusk . . . The great foot-ball ground for many years after was between Fourth and Fifth, on Chestnut. Our swimming place, when we did not go to the river, was the deep-hole in Beargrass, near Chestnut or Broadway, to reach which we had a long walk through commons and woods, beset with Paddies terrible to the straggling and lone downtowner.

Patrick Joyes, [*ca.* 1835]

62.

View of Main Street looking east from Seventh shortly after the Louisville Hotel was completed in 1834. Its innovative Greek Revival design by Hugh Roland was also functional with shops under the Ionic colonnade. A new Louisville Hotel was built on this site in 1853.

Only view of the first Galt House built in 1835 at 2nd and Main on land purchased from William C. Galt, M.D.

95.

Remodeled Galt House shortly before it burned in 1865.

96.

Doctor and naturalist Wm. Galt.

97.

64.

Belknap's, U.S. Branch Bank and Galt House are in this 1850 view of Main Street looking east from 3rd.
98.

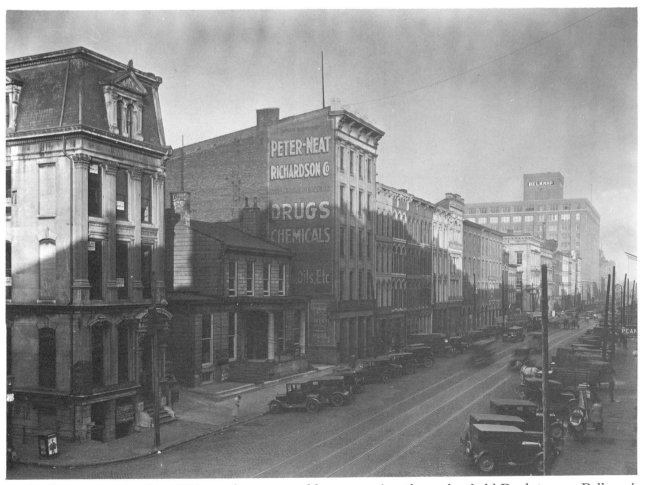

Louisville's growth by the 1920's can be measured by comparing the scale of old Bank to new Belknap's.
99.

Handsome tetrastyle Ionic portico had been removed and wings added by 1897.
100.

In 1971, the 139 year old brick and stucco Bank makes way for a parking lot.
101.

66.

Second Presbyterians built their Greek Revival church in 1832 on present 3rd St. site of the Water Company's offices.

102.

Greek Revival Unitarian Church, also built in 1832 on S.E. corner of 5th and Walnut, accommodated 650 persons.

103.

Gothic style First Presbyterian Church was
built in 1837 on site of present County Jail.

104.

English Gothic St. Paul's Episcopal Church
was also built in 1837 on 6th near Walnut.

105.

68.

Henry Clay was first to cross bridge over canal at 18th St. in 1829. Flag of Shippingport's Elm Tree Garden on right.

106.

Falls and vicinity from Clarksville *ca.* 1830. Louisville can be seen over Rock Island in center foregroun

Latrobe painted watercolor views in 1833 of the canal bridge (at left) and two types of river boats passing near the falls.

107.

Unknown artist delineated the houses and Tarascon Mill of Shippingport at right. Canal is out of view.

108.

St. Joseph Infirmary moved from Jefferson above Wenzel to 4th between Chestnut and Broadway in 1853.

109.

Additions envelope 1853 Infirmary, which had emerged from Catherine Spalding's St. Vincent Infirmary and Orphanage, begun in 1836.

110.

In view of 4th St. looking north, from a *ca.* 1910 post card, St. Joseph Infirmary is at right, old Post Office's clock tower is in center.

111.

Loew's-United Artists Theatre replaced the Infirmary which moved to its Eastern Parkway site in 1926.

112.

72.

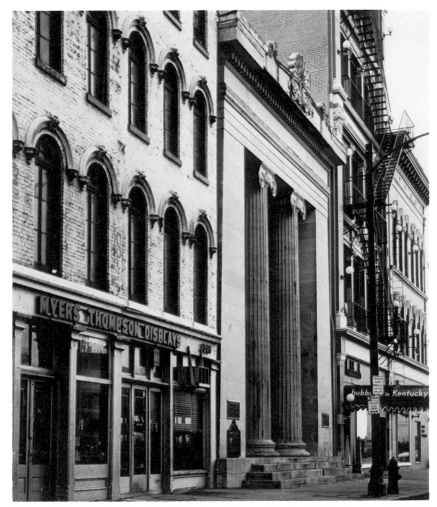
Shryock built the Bank of Louisville on Main St. between 1835-37.
113.

Classical design adapted from Lafever's plan books.
114.

Elliptical dome and skylight over old banking room.
115.

City and County built the Courthouse between 1836-42. Mayor and City officials occupied west wing.
116.

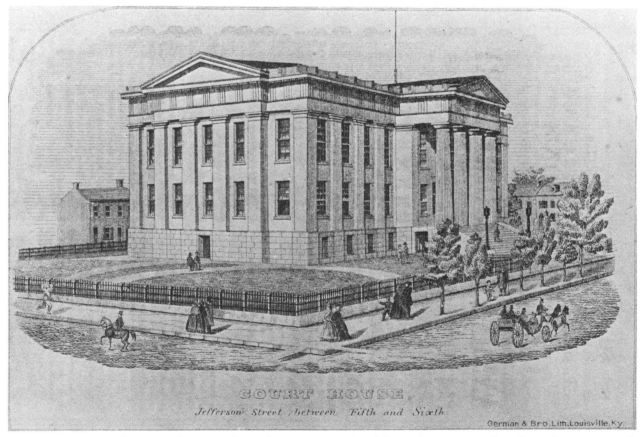

Porticoes were not built as Shryock planned. Front completed in 1858, 16 years after Courthouse opened.
117.

74.

Gideon Shryock was Kentucky's foremost architect of public buildings. From 1835-42, he built Bank of Louisville, Courthouse and Medical School, the latter two as the first City Architect.

118.

Councilman James Guthrie wanted Courthouse to become State Capitol. His career included tenures in State Legislature, as president of U. of L. and L.&N., Secretary of Treasury and U.S. Senator.

119.

This town is much larger than St. Louis, and not at all like it. The streets are as wide again. The markets are all in Market Street. There are six of them, each 400 feet long. The market houses are supported on rows of pillars about 14 feet high and nearly a foot thick in the largest part. They look exactly as if they were wood and turned in a lathe, but to my astonishment I discovered lately that they were cast iron and painted. The streets are lighted with gas. The lamp posts are iron also. The lamp[s] make the streets lighter than the full moon does, partly because the buildings obscure the light of the moon. Gas is employed in all the churches and in numerous stores and houses. The light is very brilliant and much cheaper than candles or oil. I have not yet had time to visit the gas works, but they are a great curiosity.

The Court House is superior to the Illinois State House or any other building in the West. They have been three years upon it, expended already upwards of half a million, and it is not yet half finished. You can hardly imagine any thing more splendid. The stones are not only hewed but polished. No possible expense is spared in its decoration. The cause of this enormous expense is that the people of Louisville are anxious to have the seat of government removed to this city and are building the court house for a state house and intend to present it to the state on condition of removing the seat of government. Taxes are said to be enormously high. Stores in the center of business are unoccupied. Eleven doors in a row above this office have been vacated within a week and "To Rent" is placed on them. This is the best business street in the city except Main and Market Streets which are not better. There have been several heavy failures here within a few days. Every business[man] in the U.S. has his hands full of hard times instead of hard dollars.

John Russell, 1842.

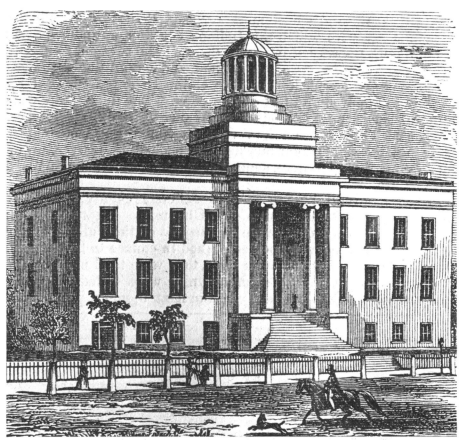

Shryock built Louisville Medical Institute at 8th and Chestnut in 1838.
120.

The Medical Institute became part of U. of L. in 1846 and occupied this site until 1909. Henry Whitestone rebuilt the burned structure in 1856.
121.

76.

E. T. Bainbridge's Row, on north side of Jefferson between 7th and 8th, reflects an 1830's housing pattern.
122.

When its residents moved, this best example of early row-housing was demolished by Urban Renewal in 1967.
123.

Waterfront from 1st to 6th was published in 1840. Back of Galt House visible at left, Presbyterian Church in background.

124.

Same view published in 1848 is not well delineated and does not indicate Beargrass Creek running behind public wharf.

125.

78.

Drum decoration shows the militia uniform worn by the Louisville Legion in 1840. Legion later fought in Mexican and Spanish-American Wars.

126.

From the ranks of the Legion, lawyer Lovell H. Rousseau raised a Union regiment which protected Louisville from Confederate invasion in 1861.

127.

Oakland Race Course at 7th and Magnolia sponsored Kentucky's first race of national importance in 1839, Grey Eagle *vs.* Wagner.

128.

During the week that we remained at Louisville, there were various causes of excitement all in action at the same time. Horse-racing, in which the Kentuckians take great delight, had drawn together a great number of sportsmen, as they are called here. A large bazaar, or fancy fair, was holding in the city, to raise funds for an orphan asylum. Bargain-making and gallantry, philanthropy and coquetry, were here strangely mingled; and all the arts of the most worldly tradespeople were put in requisition to entrap inexperienced buyers, while pious frauds were justified in the eyes of the sellers by the gains realized for charitable purposes. The theatre and the circus were at the same time crowded every night, at the benefits of favorite actors and actresses; and concerts, given at the public ball-room, were also well attended. After these, or rather contemporaneously with them, several religious meetings were held, connected with a great Baptist convention, which met here during this week, to hold its anniversary. To crown all, the city was said to be full of gamblers, this being the season at which they periodically ascend the river from New Orleans, and usually stop here for a month or two, before they scatter themselves among the fashionable watering-places, to allure their game. Many of the haunts of these gamblers were pointed out to me, and no pains were taken to conceal them. Their persons also are readily recognizable, by the greater style of fashion and expensiveness in which they dress, and the air of dissipation by which they are marked from other men. Pistols and bowie-knives are carried by them all; while their numbers, their concentrated action, and their known ferocity and determination, make them so formidable that neither the community nor the public authorities seem willing to take any bold or decisive step against them; and while lottery offices abound in all the principal streets, under the sanction or sufferance of the public, it would be difficult to justify an interference with any other kind of gambling without suppressing this at the same time.

James Silk Buckingham, 1840

80.

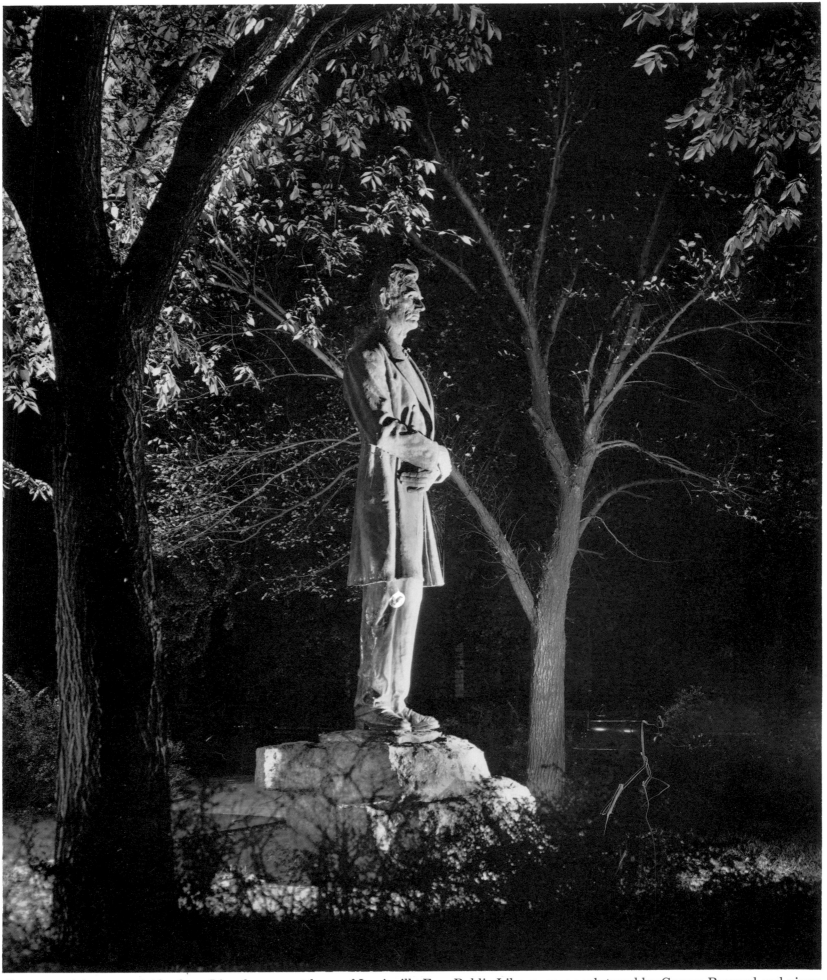

Controversial statue of Abraham Lincoln on west lawn of Louisville Free Public Library was sculptured by George Barnard and given to city by the Bernheims in 1922. Lincoln visited Farmington in 1841 to recuperate from his broken engagement to Mary Todd.

Farmington, off Bardstown Road, was finished by Judge John Speed in 1810. Federal design is believed an adaptation of Thomas Jefferson's plan. Historic Homes Foundation has operated the museum since 1958.

130.

James Speed represented Louisville in the State House and Senate before being appointed Attorney General in Lincoln's Cabinet.

131.

Joshua Fry Speed befriended Lincoln while working in Springfield, but returned to run Farmington after his father's death in 1840.

132.

The Kentucky Giant . . . had a weakness in the region of the knees, and a trustfulness in his long face, which appealed even to five-feet-nine for encouragement and support. He was only twenty-five years old, he said, and had grown recently, for it had been found necessary to make an addition to the legs of his inexpressibles. At fifteen he was a short boy, and in those days his English father and his Irish mother had rather snubbed him, as being too small of stature to sustain the credit of the family. He added that his health had not been good, though it was better now; but short people are not wanting who whisper that he drinks too hard.

I understand he drives a hackney-coach, though how he does it, unless he stands on the footboard behind, and lies along the roof upon his chest, with his chin in the box, it would be difficult to comprehend. He brought his gun with him, as a curiosity. Christened "The Little Rifle," and displayed outside a shop-window, it would make the fortune of any retail business in Holborn. When he had shown himself and talked a little while, he withdrew with this pocket-instrument, and went bobbing down the cabin, among men of six feet high and upwards, like a light-house walking among lamp-posts.

Charles Dickens, 1842.

82.

Jim Porter was 7'4" and only ninteen in 1840. He had toured the east as *the Kentucky giant*, but returned home to operate hackneys.

German & Bro.Lith,

COURT HOUSE,

Louisville, Ky.

Jefferson Street, between Fifth and Sixth.

The 1843-44 City-County Jail can be seen west (left) of the Courthouse in this 1867 engraving made prior to the erection of City Hall.

134.

1846 view of the 48-cell, Gothic Jail designed by John Jeffrey was from the Courthouse. Foreground is site of City Hall.

135.

Enlarged but outmoded Jail was replaced by City Hall Annex in 1909. Present Jail at 6th and Liberty was opened in 1905.

136.

84.

George Blanchard's clothing store at the *Sign of the Golden Hand* is seen at left, next to the Northern Bank of Kentucky located on the corner of 5th and Main. View looking west from Bullitt St. was made in 1846. Below is a broadside advertising Blanchard's wares.

137.

138.

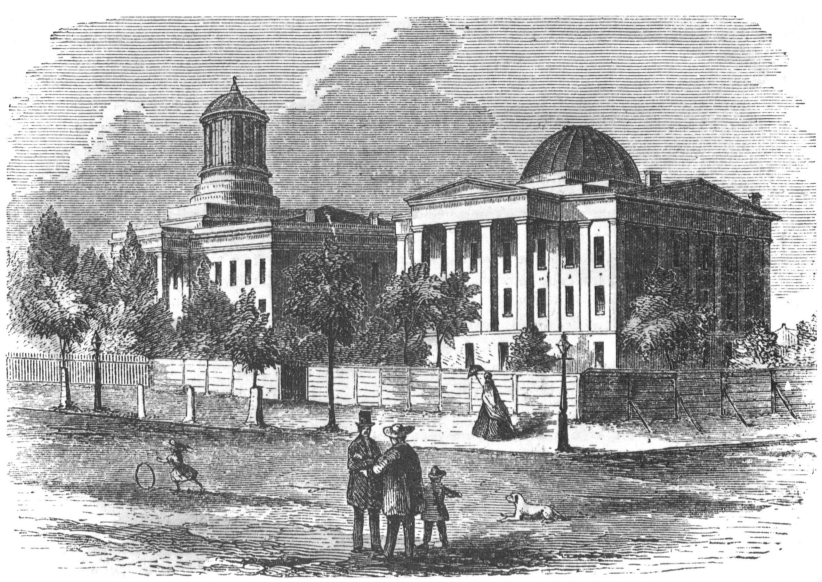

85.

U. of L. was created in 1846 on University Square. John Stirewalt completed its Academic Building next to Medical School in 1849.

139.

The Law School first occupied the Academic Building at 9th and Chestnut, then Male High School, which could grant college degrees.

140.

86.

Zachary Taylor served in the War of 1812, the Black Hawk and Seminole Wars. In 1846, *Old Rough and Ready* assumed command in the Mexican War, where victories made him popular and successful as the Whig candidate for president in 1848.

Servants' quarters on the Taylor property before its subdivision. Zachary tried to prevent sectional upheaval on slavery question.
142.

Taylor lived at Springfield from 1785 until he joined the military in 1808. Rear of private home on Apache Road is pictured in 1926.
143.

88.

After victories at Palo Alto and Monterey, Taylor disobeyed orders, moved south and defeated Santa Anna at Buena Vista in 1847.

144.

89.

1912 view of house on Brownsboro near Rebel, where Jefferson Davis, future president of the Confederacy, married Taylor's daughter.
145.

Old family graves are maintained in the Zachary Taylor National Cemetery created in 1925. State erected the memorial shaft in 1883.
146.

90.

1906 view of entrance to Cave Hill Cemetery, which was privately established on 40.6 acres granted by City in 1848.
147.

The grounds were only sparsely planted by 1889. Rest of City's Cave Hill Farm tract was used by pest and work houses.
148.

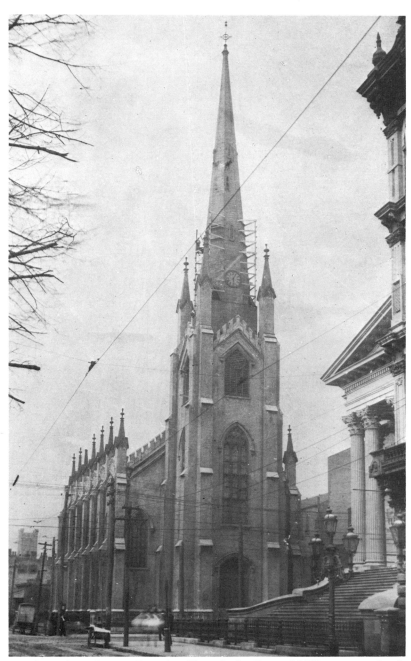

Brick Walnut Street Baptist Church, built on N.W. corner of 4th in 1853-4, was covered typically with stucco to simulate stone.

149.

The Gothic, Catholic Cathedral of the Assumption, built on 5th near Walnut in 1849-52, also had a stucco surface seen in 1897.

150.

92.

From the appearance of Louisville in the background, this romanticized view of the Falls and surrounding hills was painted about 1850.

151.

We slept at the Galt House; a splendid hotel; and were as handsomely lodged as though we had been in Paris, rather than hundreds of miles beyond the Alleghanies.

The city presenting no objects of sufficient interest to detain us on our way, we resolved to proceed next day by another steamboat, the Fulton, and to join it, about noon, at a suburb called Portland, where it would be delayed some time in passing through a canal.

The interval, after breakfast, we devoted to riding through the town, which is regular and cheerful: the streets being laid out at right angles, and planted with young trees. The buildings are smoky and blackened, from the use of bituminous coal, but an Englishman is well used to that appearance, and indisposed to quarrel with it. There did not appear to be much business stirring; and some unfinished buildings and improvements seemed to intimate that the city had been overbuilt in the ardour of "going a-head," and was suffering under the re-action consequent upon such feverish forcing of its powers.

On our way to Portland, we passed a "Magistrate's office," which amused me as looking far more like a dame school than any police establishment: for this awful Institution was nothing but a little lazy, good-for-nothing front parlour, open to the street; wherein two or three figures (I presume the magistrate and his myrmidans) were basking in the sunshine, the very effigies of languor and repose. It was a perfect picture of Justice retired from business for want of customers; her sword and scales sold off; napping comfortably with her legs upon the table.

Charles Dickens, 1842

The comparison between Louisville & Cincinnati is by no means flattering to the slave city. One notices the absence of that activity & neatness which distinguishes the former. That look of thrift & healthy progress is replaced by a sluggishness of public enterprise & a subjection of the senses, inseperable, I fear from slave labour. Here I first perceived myself in a more southern land than my native state. The physiognomy & costume assumes a more generous & liberal aspect. The sharp feautures & energetic eye & motion of the northerner & bluntness and his businesslike manner are excha[n]ged with lighter clothing for the easy contentment of manner & expression & more open social feeling of the southerner. One still bears the marks of his puritan origin while the cavalier still glimmers thro' the southern planter's exterior. This case of manner & hospitality thro' traits greatly to be admired and imitated do not compensate for the want of public energy & enterprise which is so nobly exhibited in the sister city of Cincinnati.

Frank Blackwell Mayer, 1851

Anglo-Norman Customs House was erected in 1851 at 3rd and Liberty for $258,500. Post Office was on ground floor.

152.

1865 engraving of the Masonic Temple which stood on the S.W. corner of 4th and Jefferson from 1852 until 1903.

153.

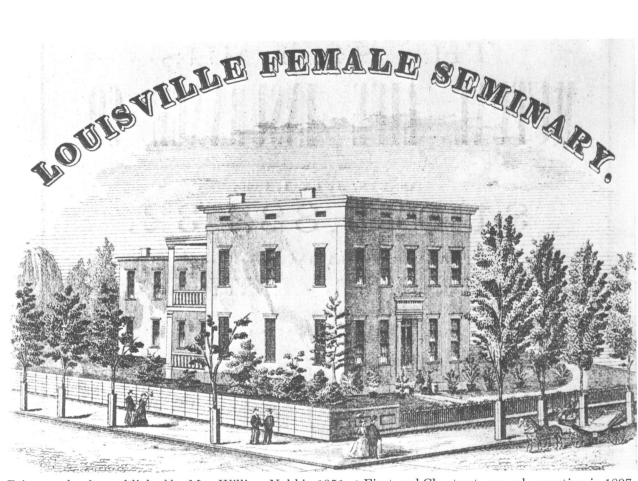

Private school, established by Mrs. William Nold in 1851 at First and Chestnut, ceased operating in 1897.

154.

94.

1859 engraving of the First Ward School established in 1853 on Market near Wenzel, later known as Margaret Merker School until 1966.

155.

95.

Ca. 1870 photograph by Klauber, looking down Gray to intersection of Shelby. The Church of St. Martin's of Tours was built in 1853-54.

96.

Waterfront view, published in *Gleason's Pictorial Drawing-Room Companion* of 2 Sept. 1854, shows four modes of river transportation.

157.

Beargrass Creek still entered the Ohio between 3rd and 4th in *circa* 1855 view published as a letterhead by Charles Magnus of New York.

158.

This view of Louisville from Jeffersonville appeared in the *Ladies' Repository* of 1854. It was the basis for the 1856 engraving below.
159.

This imaginative proposal for the *Great Tunnel* with dual transportation tubes did not materialize and bridges were built across Ohio.
160.

98.

This scene of the public landing in 1856 is probably the most explicit view ever made of stevedores loading boats along the wharf.
161.

French version of waterfront and bridge over Beargrass Creek at 2nd St. illustrated the journal of Comettant's 1859 trip to America.
162.

This *circa*. 1850 view in *Lloyd's Steamboat Directory* . . . of 1856 aptly demonstrates the time lag usually found in early publications.
163.

99.

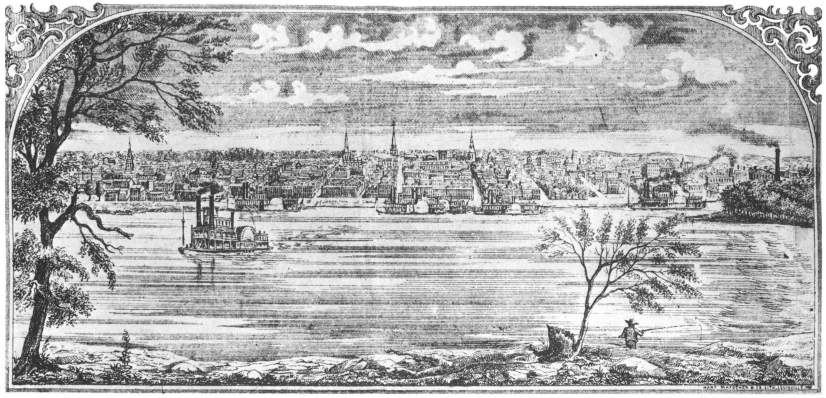

A well-delineated adaptation of the above appeared in *Edward's Annual Directory* of 1864-65. Catholic Cathedral on 5th St. is in center.
164.

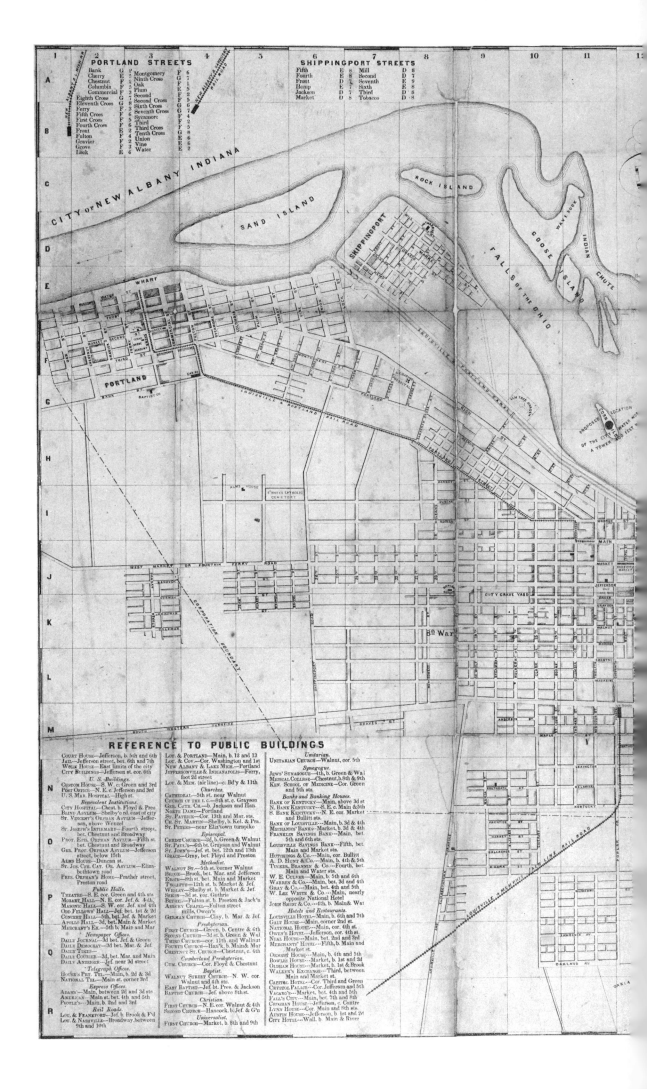

A NEW MAP OF LOUISVILLE KY.

PUBLISHED BY W. LEE WHITE,

from Hart & Mapothers large Map.

Hart & Mapother Sc.

EXPLANATION

...the name of the Street wanted, in the ...h the initial and figure, then find the ...ding initial on the left of the Map ...race the map until you come under ...the same figure.

—1856—

Scale 4 inches to a Mile

LOUISVILLE STREETS

Albert	K 5	Clay	L 18	Gray	L 16	Marshall	K 7	Prather	M 13	Spurrier	I 17
Adams	H 21	Clinton	G 21	Grayson	K 11	Maria	N 9	Prentice	Q 9	Third	L 14
Anderson	M 9	Clinton or 19th	L 9	Green	K 11	Mary	O 19	Preston	L 16	Tenth	L 12
Arthur	N 16	Coleman	K 3	Guthrie	K 15	Mechanic	O 17	Quarry	J 23	Twelfth	L 11
Arthur W	K 5	College	M 15	Hanover	J 3	Milk	P 18	Quincy	P 19	Thirteenth	K 11
Bayard	Q 13	Charlton	J 23	Herman	K 3	Missouri	M 14	Rowan	I 8	Twentieth	J 8
Beargrass	H 22	De Wolf or 18th	L 9	Harney	L 9	Monroe	I 11	Russell Ave.	M 23	Twenty-First	J 7
Boone or 14th	L 10	Delaware	N 11	Harney N	I 8	Montgomery	H 8	Rose Lane	L 8	Twenty-Second	J 7
Brady	I 17	Duncan	I 8	High	G 9	Mott	Q 12	Rothwell	P 15	Twenty-Third	J 7
Broadway	M 12	Dumesnil	P 11	Irvine	L 16	Mulberry	G 20	Salnglo	M 17	Twenty-Fourth	J 7
Brook	I 16	East	K 15	Jackson	L 17	Maple	M 10	Sefull	K 6	Twenty-Fifth	J 6
Breckenridge	N 15	Edward	M 20	Jacob	M 15	Mill	H 19	Second	L 15	Twenty-Sixth	J 6
Bridge	H 9	Eighth	L 13	Jefferson	J 11	Nelson	J 13	Seventeenth	K 9	Thorn	I 21
Buchanan	I 13	Elizabeth	O 10	John	K 11	Nineteenth	K 9	Seventh	L 13	Thomas	M 11
Bullitt	I 14	Eighteenth	K 9	Kellar	K 3	Ninth	L 18	Sixteenth	L 12	Underhill	L 20
Campbell	L 19	Elder	I 21	Kentucky	N 11	Oak	P 12	Short	J 12	Van Buren	G 20
Cabell	H 20	Eleventh	L 12	Lafayette	I 18	Oakland Ave.	K 16	Sixteenth	K 10	Vine	M 17
Campbell S	O 16	Elm	H 18	Lampton	M 17	O'Hara	O 9	Sixth	L 13	Walnut	K 11
Canal	G 22	Fifteenth	L 10	Lawrence Ave.	Q 11	Ohio	G 21	Slaughter Ave.	M 23	Water	I 13
Cane	O 19	Fifth	L 14	Locust	J 22	Ormsby	I 12	Southgate	K 3	Wayne	I 20
Caldwell	N 16	First	L 15	Lombard	G 20	Ormsby Ave.	P 12	Stokes' Ave.	K 9	Wayne, ov. Cr'k	G 20
Centre	L 14	Floyd	L 16	Laurel	L 16	Orchill	L 21	Stone	I 16	Washington	I 16
Caroline	M 21	Fulton	H 18	Lexington	N 11	Payne	I 21	Southall	I 22	Webster	I 21
St. Catharine	O 14	Fourth	L 14	Lloyd	I 18	Pearl	G 21	Spring	I 22	Wenzel	K 49
Cawthon	M 12	Franklin	I 18	Madison	K 11 17	Pery	I 14	St. Louis	I 17	West	M 10
Chapel	J 12	Garden	K 19	Magazine	L 11	Pochahontas	L 11	Sewart Ave.	I 26	Weisinger Ave.	Q 13
Cherry	O 10	Gallagher	O 9	Main E	I 21	Pope	N 14	St. Bernard	I 22	Wood	G 20
Chestnut	L 11	Geiger	J 19	Maiden Lane	H 21	Portland Ave.	G 7	St. Joseph	I 14	Woodbine	Q 16
Christy Ave.	M 21	Grauman	K 3	Marion	H 21	Portland	H 8	Sycamore	L 9		
Clark or 15th	L 10	Graves	M 7	Market	J 11	Poplar	J 11	Scend	O 12	York	M 12

OHIO RIVER

CITY OF JEFFERSONVILLE

165.

102.

1856 view of Beargrass Creek just before this section along Ohio was filled in. Bridge was at Preston and gas holders on Washington were part of the oldest Gas Works in the West.

166.

Scene in Cherokee Park taken in 1907. Beargrass was frequently navigated in pioneer days.

167.

1856 view looking south on 6th at intersection of Green (Liberty) Street. First Presbyterian Church at left now site of Jail.

168.

DuPonts dug a 2,000 foot artesian well near Tenth St. and Ohio River in 1858. It could raise water 170 feet above ground.

169.

Speed Market between 5th and 6th was one of five enclosed produce stands along Market St. in 1856. Note pigs in the foreground.

170.

Here, as elsewhere in these parts, the [Portland] road was perfectly alive with pigs of all ages; lying about in every direction, fast asleep; or grunting along in quest of hidden dainties. I had always a sneaking kindness for these odd animals, and found a constant source of amusement, when all others failed, in watching their proceedings. As we were riding along this morning, I observed a little incident between two youthful pigs, which was so very human as to be inexpressibly comical and grotesque at the time, though I daresay, in telling, it is tame enough.

One young gentleman (a very delicate porker with several straws sticking about his nose, betokening recent investigations in a dung-hill), was walking deliberately on, profoundly thinking, when suddenly his brother, who was lying in a miry hole unseen by him, rose up immediately before his startled eyes, ghostly with damp mud. Never was pig's whole mass of blood so turned. He started back at least three feet, gazed for a moment, and then shot off as hard as he could go: his excessively little tail vibrating with speed and terror like a distracted pendulum. But before he had gone very far, he began to reason with himself as to the nature of this frightful appearance; and as he reasoned, he relaxed his speed by gradual degrees; until at last he stopped, and faced about. There was his brother, with the mud upon him glazing in the sun, yet staring out of the very same hole, perfectly amazed at his proceedings! He was no sooner assured of this; and he assured himself so carefully that one may almost say he shaded his eyes with his hand to see the better; than he came back at a round trot, pounced upon him, and summarily took off a piece of his tail; as a caution to him to be careful what he was about for the future, and never to play tricks with his family any more.

Charles Dickens, 1842

The classical Louisville Water Works on River Rd. was designed and built by T. R. Scowden between 1856-60.

171.

Costigan finished the splendid Greek Revival building, Kentucky School for the Blind, on Frankfort Ave. in 1855.

172.

Panorama of the Western Agricultural and Mechanical Association's amphitheater on its Fair Grounds in Crescent Hill is created by juxtaposing

106.

THE TENT.—[FROM A PHOTOGRAPH BY WEBSTER AND BROTHER, LOUISVILLE.]

Amphitheater seated 10,000 spectators around a one mile track. Tent housed fair officials and press.

174.

Accessible by railroad or turnpike, the Grou

engravings published in a September 1857 newspaper. Livestock show was part of the fifth exhibition of the United States Agricultural Society.
173.

so had a Power Hall (above) and Floral Hall.
175.

THE MACHINERY HALL.—[FROM A PHOTOGRAPH BY WEBSTER AND BROTHER.]

Cider mills were prominently displayed. Engravings were from photos by Webster and Brother.
176.

108.

Incensed mob, moving west on Jefferson to the old Jail (site of City Hall Annex), hung 4 acquitted of murder in 1857.

177.

The defeated American (Know-Nothing) party held its 1857 convention in Mozart Hall on N.E. corner of 4th and Jefferson.

178.

109.

1859 lithograph of Bannon's ornamental terra cotta works located on 5th adjacent to present site of Founders Square.

110.

This beautifully delineated lithograph, made from a *circa* 1857 ambrotype, is the most realistic street scene before the use of fast camer

111.

...wn are the Breckenridge Block at left and four other store-houses at right on the south side of Main, east of Third. Note old street numbering system.

112.

Three-story buildings still predominate along Main. Scene looking east from 4th, *circa*. 1855.

181.

By 1889, the character of Main east of 4th had completely changed, especially the sign advertising.

182.

Earliest extant Louisville photograph is a *ca.* 1858 ambrotype of north side of Main, west of Bullitt.
183.

Few changes took place along Main St. in next 30 years, except the omnibus was replaced by trolleys.
184.

114.

Lithograph of Orpheus Society, a male chorus once popular in city's large German community, was made from an 1860 ambrotype

del & lith

Ambrotypes by A. McG.ll

Formed in 1849, the Orpheus Society was only prosperous during the 1860's and 70's, and then evidently its members disbanded.

116.

The pro-Secessionist State Guard held its first encampment on the County Fair Grounds in August, 1860.

186.

Flags expressed Union sentiment. Home Guard was led by city's best-known Union soldier, Genl. Rousseau.

187.

Walter N. Haldeman strongly espoused Southern causes in his *Louisville Daily Courier*, until it was suppressed.

188.

George D. Prentice was Louisville's most influential political writer. His *Journal* expounded the pro-Union view.

189.

Soldiers of Old Kentuck,
"MOTTO",
We live for the Union.
We die for the Union.
We will uphold the Union.

The majority of Louisville's citizens, like Prentice, advocated preserving the Union, but ironically, supported continuing slavery too.

190.

118.

Threatened for the first time by a Confederate thrust into Kentucky, city welcomed the arrival of Union troops in September 1861.

191.

City was assembling area for Union troops in late 1861. Fort Sumter hero, Robt. Anderson gave up command to Wm. Tecumseh Sherman.

192.

After Buell succeeded Sherman in late 1861, his headquarters were on the west side of 4th near Walnut. Catholic Cathedral is in background.

193.

General Don Carlos Buell trained about 80,000 Union troops massed in and around Louisville, before he ordered them south in February 1862.

194.

120.

Believing a Confederate invasion by Braxton Bragg's forces was imminent, Genl. Nelson ordered women and children to evacuate. Henri Lo

orded the hectic departure for Indiana on 22 Sept. 1862. When Bragg halted in Bardstown, Buell's troops slipped back into Louisville to protect it.

Henry Mosler sketched a more orderly departure of citizens for *Harper's Weekly*. Second Street is at left.
196.

Union Genl. Samuel Curtis' division marches past cheering throng on the balcony of the new Louisville Hotel.
197.

Buell's bodyguard is parading east on Main at 5th St. in January 1862, shortly before moving south, leaving the city unprotected.

198.

Buell's army, which raced back into city on 25 Sept. along the Salt River Rd. (Dixie Highway), is seen on Broadway, east of 18th St.

199.

124.

NEW YORK
ILLUSTRATED NEWS.

No. 154.—Vol. VI. NEW-YORK, SATURDAY, OCTOBER 18, 1862. PRICE SIX CENTS.

THE SHOOTING OF GENERAL NELSON, AT THE GALT HOUSE, LOUISVILLE, KY., BY GEN. JEFF. C. DAVIS. FROM A SKETCH BY OUR SPECIAL ARTIST, J. C.

Dismissed for insubordination, Genl. Jefferson C. Davis confronted his superior, Genl. Wm. "Bull" Nelson on Sept. 29th. When Nelson walked away, unarmed, Davis shot and killed him, but was never tried.

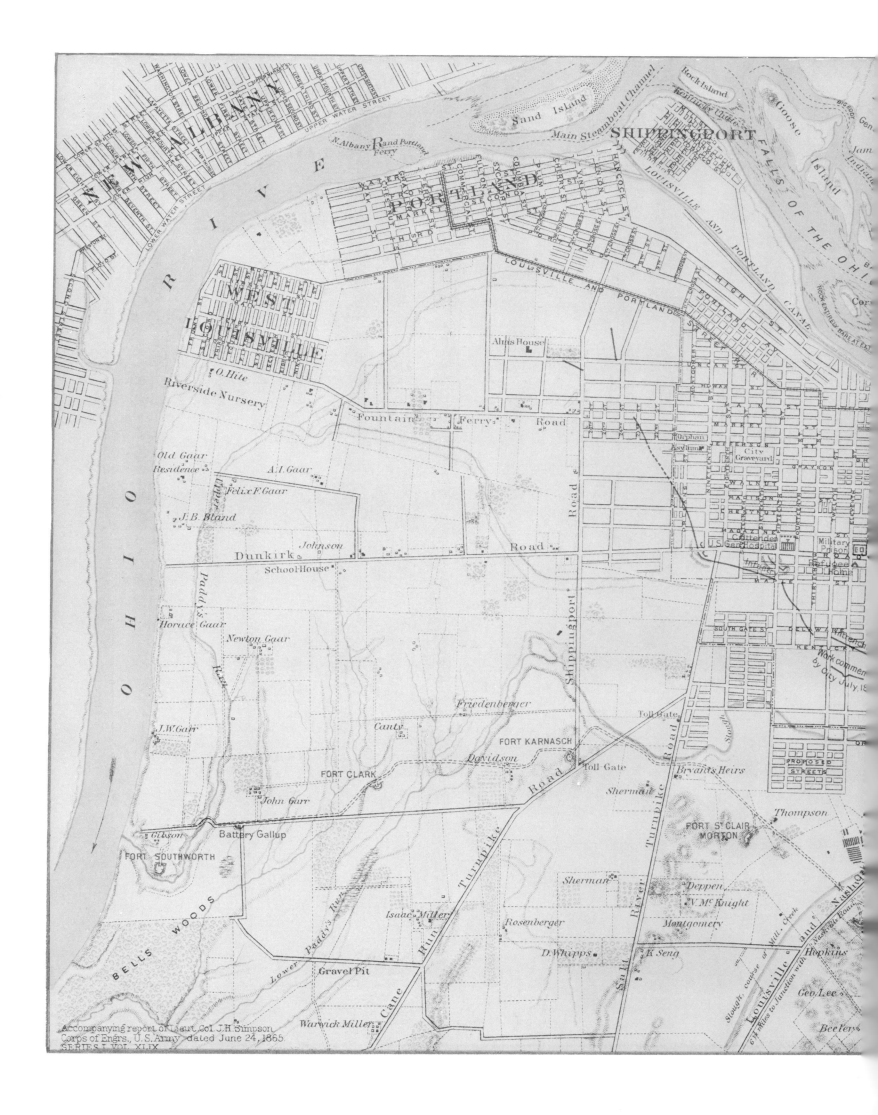

NEW ALBANY

PORTLAND

SHIPPINGPORT

FALLS OF THE OHIO

WEST LOUISVILLE

R I V E R

O H I O

Sand Island

Rock Island

Goose Island

Main Steamboat Channel

LOUISVILLE AND PORTLAND CANAL

N. Albany and Portland Ferry

LOUISVILLE AND PORTLAND

O. Hite

Riverside Nursery

Alms House

Fountain Ferry Road

Old Gaar Residence

A. I. Gaar

Felix F. Gaar

City Graveyard

J. B. Bland

Johnson

Dunkirk

Road

Road

School-House

U.S. Gen. Hospital

Military Prison

Horace Gaar

Newton Gaar

Shippingport

Friedenberger

J. W. Gaar

Canty

Toll Gate

FORT KARNASCH

Davidson

Bryants Heirs

FORT CLARK

Toll Gate

Sherman

John Garr

Thompson

Gibson

Battery Gallup

FORT ST. CLAIR MORTON

FORT SOUTHWORTH

Sherman

Deppen

V. McKnight

BELLS WOODS

Rosenberger

Montgomery

Isaac Miller

D. Whipps

K. Seng

Hopkins

Lower Paddy's Run

Gravel Pit

Geo. Lee

Warwick Miller

Cane Run

Salt River

Beelers

Turnpike Road

Turnpike Road

LOUISVILLE AND NASHVILLE

Accompanying report of Lieut. Col. J. H. Simpson
Corps of Engrs., U.S. Army dated June 24, 1865.
SERIES I VOL. XLIX

3.

127.

From plan of City by Hart and
Mapother; Plots of land surveys
by G.T. Bergman, County Surveyor,
and surveys made by order of
Lieut. Col. J.H. Simpson under the
direction of John R. Gilliss Asst.
U.S. Engr by J.M. Hamilton and
W.J. Gilliss, and Geo. B. Nicholson.
Fortifications constructed by
order of Major Gen. J.M. Schofield,
Commanding Department of the Ohio
under the direction of Lieut. Col.
J.H. Simpson, Corps of Engineers,
by John R. Gilliss, Asst U.S. Engr,
Assisted by Ernst Riihl Asst U.S.
Engr.
Commenced, August 1st, 1864.
Finished
Drawn by ROB. G. PHILLIPS
From original map compiled by
G. B. Nicholson.

REFERENCES:
Government Buildings
Military Roads
McAdamized Roads
Dirt Roads
Railroad
Brick Houses
Frame Houses
Old Infantry Intrenchments
New Infantry Intrenchments
Churches
Fences
Distances on Roads measured
from Court-House.

LOUISVILLE
AND ITS
DEFENSES.

SCALE OF FEET

| 1000 | 0 | 1000 | 2000 | 3000 | 4000 | 5000 | 6000 |

SCALE OF YARDS

SCALE OF MILES

Union

Office U.S. Engineers,
Cincinnati, O.
June, 1865.
official
J.H. Simpson,
Lt Col. Engrs. U.S. Army.

202.

View over Brown General Hospital at emplacements of Fort McPherson, route of North-South Expwy. from Eastern Pkwy. to Barbee.
203.

Only five photographs of the vast Union installations in and around Louisville are now extant. They were taken probably in late 1864.
204.

The seven wards of the Crittenden U.S. General Hospital are being completed and painted on the N.E. corner of 15th and Broadway.
205.

Commissary warehouse cannot be located. It may have replaced storehouses between 8th and 9th on Main which burned in July 1864.

206.

New barracks appear to be on Broadway, west of Crittenden Hospital at far right. 15th St. was cut through entrenchment excavations.

207.

John C. Fremont's fleet of gunboats enabled Buell to control all river traffic below Louisville by late 1861. City is in background.
208.

Ironclads were able to pass over the falls at high water in 1866. The waterfront's lower landing is seen extending to Shippingport.
209.

I do not know what year it was, but it was after the birthday party [1841], I remember, seeing men digging a long hole in the street in front of our house, in which they laid down and covered up a lot of work pipe, that I was told was to bring gas, to light lamps on the streets; and they laid smaller pipes into our house, and ran those pipes into all the rooms, and you could take your fingers and turn a little cock, and hold a piece of burning wood or paper over the place where the bad-smelling gas was coming out, with a hissing noise, and we at once had a beautiful light, that soon drove away the use of whale-oil and lard oil lamps, and candles. And then at the time of the day the almanac said the sun was down, even if he wasn't, or the moon was not shining, boys working for the Gas Company ran along the sidewalks, with light ladders on their shoulders and stopping at the gas lamp posts on the corners, would run up the ladder, turn the stop cock, hold a lantern for a moment over the gas, and when it was lighted drop down and run along to the next one. And in the early morning, though it might still be as dark as night, these boys ran around and put out the gas, because the almanac said it was broad daylight. . . .

I have seen many different kinds of street pavements. At first all the streets that were paved were macadamized — that reminds me, I can recall, when there was no street pavement on Broadway except each side of a nice little park in that street, between Sixth and Seventh Streets. McAdam gave way to boulders, taken from the bottom of the Ohio River — I think the first came from Rising Sun bar — away up beyond Madison. And then it was found that Twelve Mile Island bar gave just as good, and maybe other places. Brook Street gave up in 1916 boulder pavement put down long before the Civil War. I know the boulder part of High Avenue, if there is any left, was put down in 1857. Then some Michigan promoters came here and got permission to put down a square of Nicholson pavement, of pine blocks saturated with coal tar, on Jefferson Street, between Fifth and Sixth Streets, which became a regular resort for those of our wealthy citizens who had handsome horses and carriages, to drive up and down that square and 'show off'. Then the boulder pavements in the business parts of the city where the hauling was the heaviest, gave way in many sections to Georgia granite, and brick and it to asphalt, and that to the wood again.

When I first remember, our cooking stove burned wood, and when the Pond settlement, that is the section down on the Salt River Road now 18th Street, between Louisville and Salt River, was covered with dense woods, stove wood was cheap and of the best kinds of hard woods, ash and beech. We had a large shed for holding wood, a smaller house for coal for the parlor and dining room, but the wood finally gave way to the Pittsburg coal, which was the only kind for a long time, being floated here many years before the adaptation of the steamboat to push the boats down the river.

There was also an industry which has disappeared entirely, and that was rafting pine lumber and pine logs to Louisville, that came from the forests along the Allegheny, and its tributaries, now the forests have been cleared, the hills cultivated, and the capital invested otherwise, For many years all the white pine used in housebuilding, steamboat construction and a thousand different ways, came to us by water as I have said. . . .

And we were a happy people then, if we did not have any but Macadam streets that were muddy all winter and dusty all summer. And we had no street cars, or steam fire engines or telephones, or telegraphs and the darkies were a large share of the people, but not a large share of the criminals. And the police were watchmen, and wore no uniforms, though at night they were armed and each had a big stick. And the boys were boys, even as they are now, and delighted in playing the same old jokes they do now. And tho there were men and women who drank whisky, the crimes from such a cause were seldom such tragedies as we have now. And the men were always polite and chivalrous toward a woman, no matter who she was, old or young, rich or poor. Perhaps 'distance lends enchantment to the view', but this City was a more attractive home than it is now.

Alfred Pirtle, 1917

Marcellus Jerome Clarke, alias Sue Mundy, notorious leader of a marauding band in Kentucky, hanged in Louisville on 15 March 1865.

132.

133.

painting of Falls with an industralized Louisville in background was made by Alexander Wyant in 1863.

134.

1 Geo. Zoeller	8 Geo. Baum	15 A. Huber	22 Wm Geissel	29 Geo. J. Buckstuhl	36 Jos. Taufkirch
2 C. Funke	9 P. Meier	16 J. C. Hunt	23 F. Pfisterer	30 F. Ileser	37 F. W. M. Schön
3 Jos. Isert	10 F. Walter	17 G. Müller	24 Geo. Zubrod	31 A. Stein	38 St. Schreind
4 G. Kick	11 G. S. Schuhmann	John. Ehrmann	25 Ph. Altenburger	32 Ch. Winkler	39 W. Hoch
5 J. M. Kremm	12 J. M. Landsrath	18 A. Jespies	26 Wm Ruby	33 Jos. Pyscher	40 Geo. Wolf
6 Geo. A. Ehrmann	13 J. Doerr	20 J. G. Knapper	27 Fr. Ruby	34 C. Kamm	41 Ch. Bartels
7 C. Scheffel	14 C. Oehlmann	21 C. Widler	28 Ch. Holzhewner	35 G. Schulz	42 Geo. Hermann

LIE
Lo

135.

RANZ

1865.

43. E. Sauermann	50. H. Seib	57. Wm Ehrmann	64. Jos Wolf	71. F. Volkmar	78. C. Stege
44. A. Nense	51. G. Gelfus	58. C. Mühlenschläger	65. C. Holderegger	72. C. Brenner	79. E. Ehrmann
46. R. Dorn	52. Wm Noller	59. A. Stützel	66. F. Schaub	73. J. Friess	80. C. Meier
47. John Voelker	53. F.F. Pfrommer	60. E. Husemann	67. G.H. Laib	74. J. Bossung	81. C. Springer
48. A. Zimmermann	54. L. Eisenkremer	61. F. Zell	68. L. Ehrmann	75. F. Schwenk	82. Ed. Rapp
49. C. Bitner	55. R. Mausfeld	62. G. Schuster	69. C. Reis	76. W. Wichelmann	83. Jos. Haxthausen
	56. M. Billing	63. C. Schneider	70. F. Weihe	77. Geo. Duell	84. F. Springer

136.

A youthful Western Union telegraph operator, Thomas A. Edison, left Louisville in 1866 when he was fired for experimenting.
213.

Edison lived two years at 729 E. Washington. He returned in 1883 to install his new electric lamps in the Southern Exposition.
214.

137.

The Confederate Monument was erected in 1895 on 3rd St. near the House of Refuge. Ferdinand von Miller of Munich cast the sentinels.

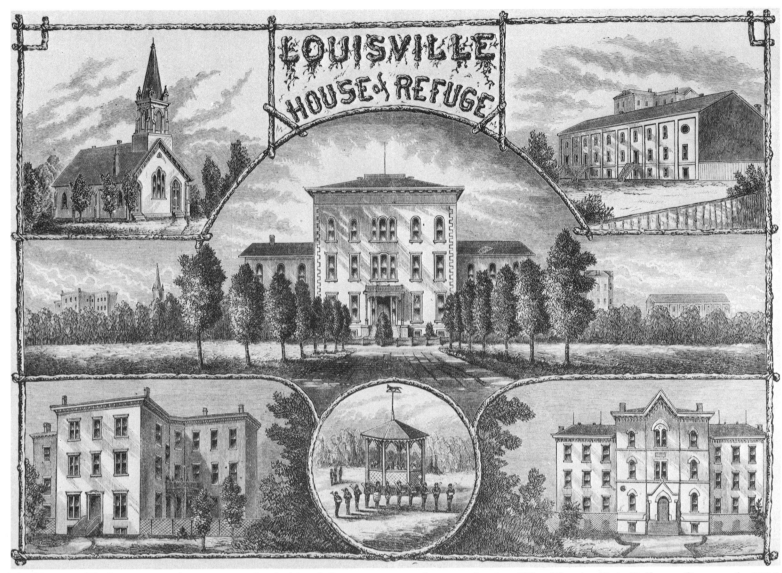

The House of Refuge, opened in 1866 on the Oakland Cemetery tract, became basis of U. of Louisville's Belknap Campus in 1924.

216.

Later known as the Industrial Reform School, its main building burned in 1924 and was replaced by the J. B. Speed Art Museum.

217.

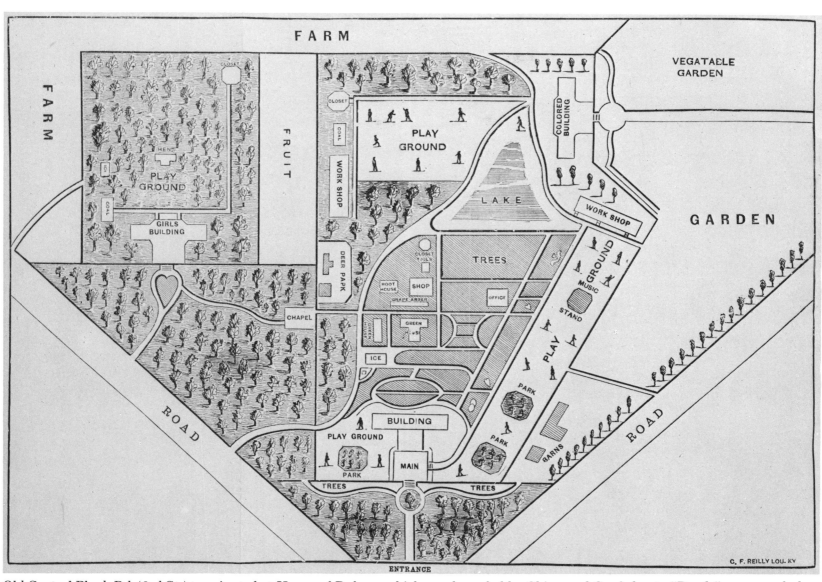

Old Central Plank Rd. (3rd St.) terminated at House of Refuge, which was bounded by Shipp and Confederate "Roads" on ground plan.

218.

139.

In 1928, U. of L. had lots of land on Eastern Pkwy. for expansion.

219.

Spectators watch 3rd St. underpass (at left) being built in 1930.

220.

140.

1867 scene of activity around the Adams Express Co. on the west side of Sixth St. between Market and Main.

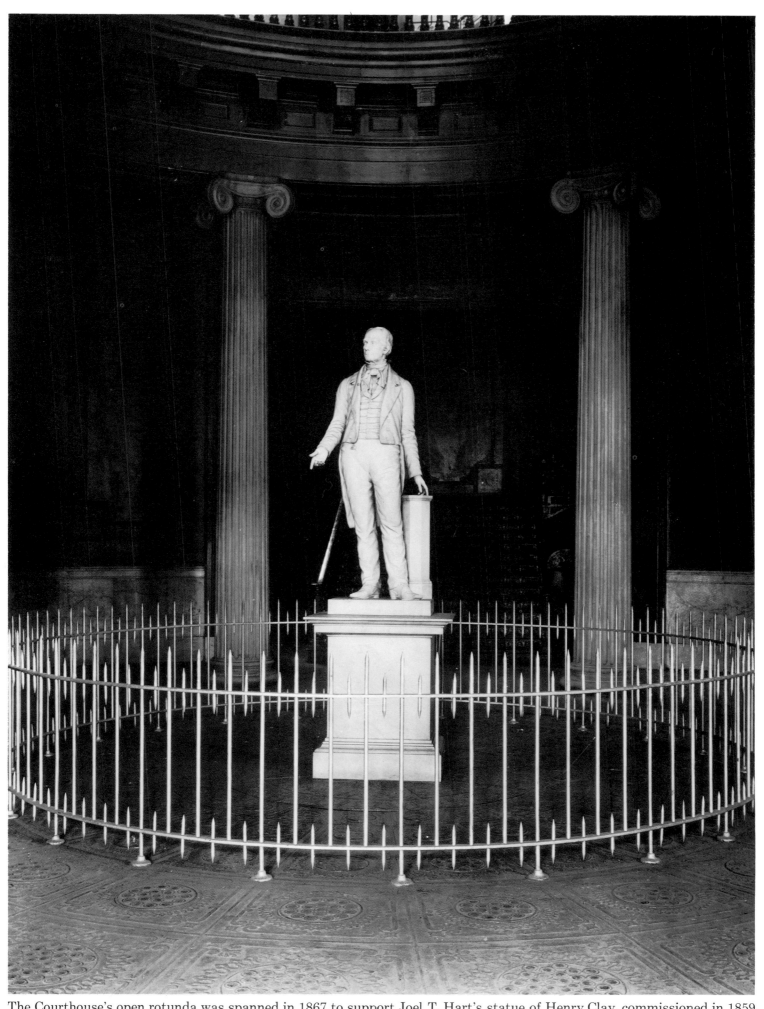

141.

The Courthouse's open rotunda was spanned in 1867 to support Joel T. Hart's statue of Henry Clay, commissioned in 1859.

Temple Adas Israel, built on S.E. corner of 6th and Broadway in 1868 and later used by Methodists, now is a parking lot.

223.

The Temple can be seen on Broadway, west of old Greyhound Station, which is under construction and water of the 1937 flood.

224.

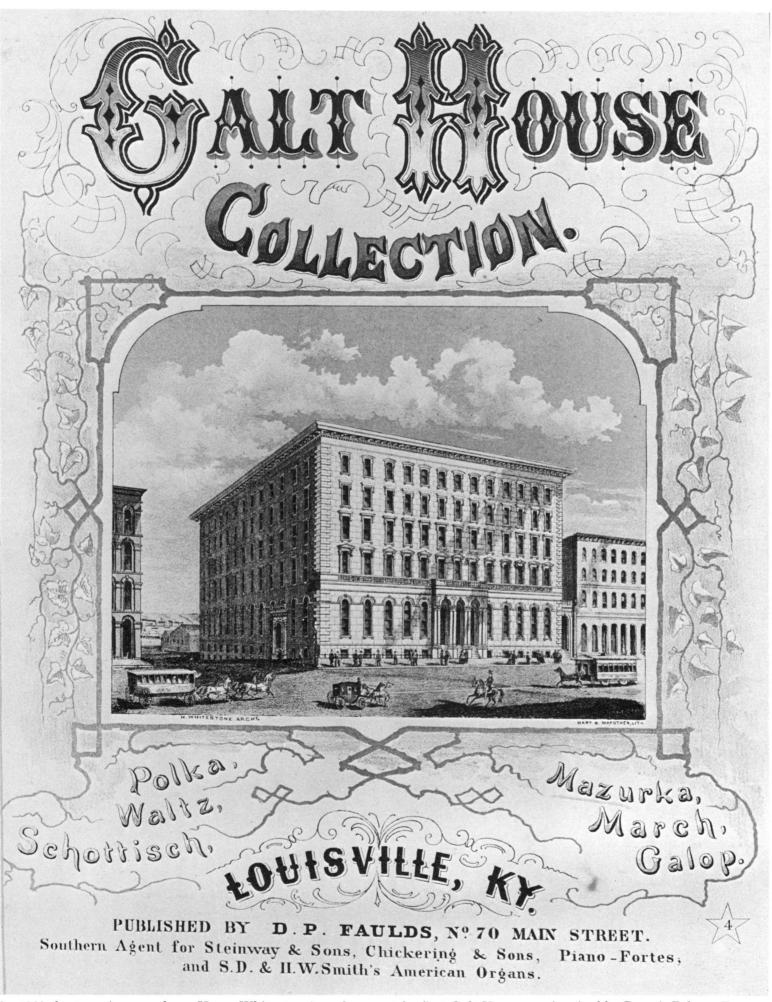

An 1869 sheet music cover shows Henry Whitestone's replacement for first Galt House was inspired by Rome's Palazzo Farnese.

144.

Photograph of baggage wagons outside the second Galt House was probably made in early 1870's.

226.

Entrance to Galt House, built on N.E. corner of 1st and Main between 1865-69 and razed in 1921.

227.

"OUR OWN"

Entered according to Act of Congress, in the year 1869, by J. S. McMAIN, in the Clerk's Office in the District Court of Kentucky.

Photographed by (COURIER-JOURNAL PRINT.) E. Klauber.

145.

"Our Own" brand made a unique tobacco label, containing an early Edward Klauber photo of its cigar inspection.

146.

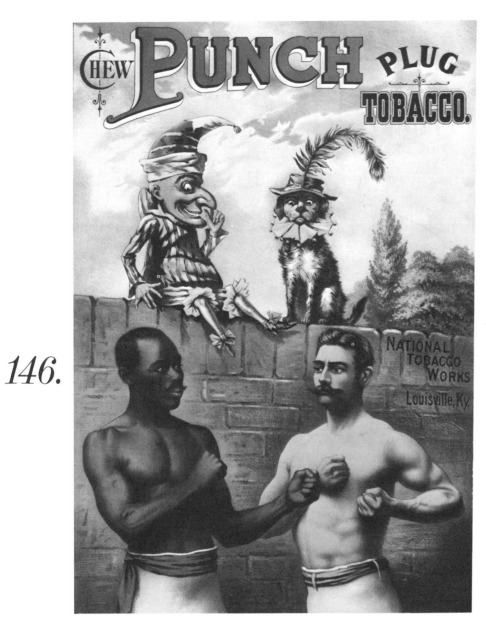

229.

230.

Prior to auctions, tobacco buyers were permitted to examine exposed hogsheads, a feature which made Louisville's market largest in world.
231.

For decades, tobacco was brought for auction to warehouses along Main St., west of 9th, in the same way shown in these 1906 photos.
232.

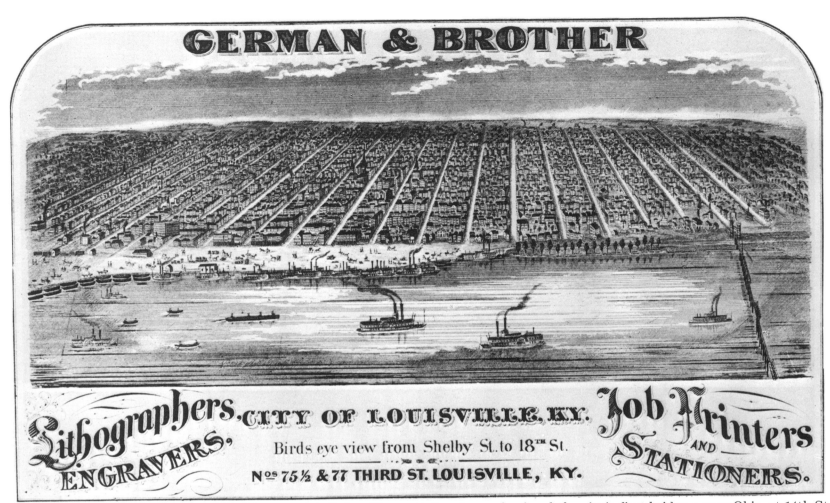

Advertisement published in the 1870 *Directory* details bustling activity along wharf and the city's first bridge across Ohio, at 14th St.

233.

An 1874 engraving shows a side-wheeler passing under a channel span, patented by Albert Fink, who built the bridge between 1868-70.

234.

City's waterfront is framed by the almost 100 foot high span of the Ohio Falls Bridge over the Indiana Chute in *ca.* 1870 photograph.
235.

149.

On 12 February 1870, Klauber photographed the first passenger trains crossing over the 27 spans of the mile long, $2 million bridge.
236.

Louisville and Portland Canal had a depth of only 3 feet at low water when first built.

150.

By the 1850's, almost half the boats on western waters could not get through the Canal.
238.

National Archives' photos (above) show the enlarging and lock work done in early 1870's.
239.

Locks and Dam 41 was later named for District Engineer W. H. McAlpine. New Dam was built between 1961-64.
240.

1923 view before hydroelectric plant, finished in 1930. Canal was improved with new locks between 1959-65.
241.

152.

he Canal was being widened and a coffer dam built when photographed by Klauber in 1873. The waterfront, east of 6th St., is in the background.

154.

243.

Interior of the Exposition on the N.E. corner of 4th and Chestnut.

244.

Industrial expositions were held until U.S. purchased site in 1883.

245.

In the late 1880's, U.S. built the magnificent Renaissance Revival Post Office and Custom House on the Exposition's site.

Entrance to Louisville and Portland Canal in 1873 and channel dredge tied up at the foot of 8th St. probably because of the high water.

247.

156.

This section of the public wharf evidently had not been paved yet when sporting stevedores churned up dust racing their tandems in 1871.

248.

Two-wheeled wagons were not eliminated from levee scene until advent of mechanized transportation. Photograph published in 1902.

249.

The Liederkranz Society erected its first recital hall in 1872 at 172 Market Street, but soon after had to relinquish it.

250.

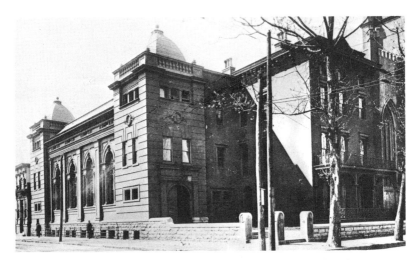

Regrouped financially, the Society built a second hall in 1896 at 6th and Walnut. It would later house the "Hollywood Follies."

251.

158.

[READING ROOM.] [ART GALLERY.]

$422,396, from five lotteries, endowed the Library and renovated the Central Market on east side of 4th between Liberty and Walnut.

252.

The Public Library of Kentucky
was incorporated by the Legislature of Kentucky March 16th, 1871. The charter required the Library to be located in Louisville, to be open every day and night in the year and to be forever free to all citizens. To raise the means to establish and sustain a Library on such a plan the Trustees were authorized to give five literary musical or dramatic entertainments, at which they might distribute by lot to patrons of the entertainments a portion of the proceeds, arising from the sale of tickets of admission. They organized under the charter March 22d, 1871 and determined that the five entertainments should be Gift-Concerts. Two of the Concerts have already been given and with the money derived therefrom an ample lot fronting 168 feet on 4th Street, between Green and Walnut, having a depth of 200 feet entirely covered by a magnificent building, four stories high, in the Renaissance style of architecture was purchased January 27th 1872 at a cost of $210,000. In this building the Trustees have already placed a Library of 40,000 volumes and a Museum of 250,000 specimens, which were formally opened to the public April 27th, 1872. It is expected from the remaining Concerts to increase the Library and Museum to many times their present capacity, to open a gallery of Art and Academy of design, to publish a strictly literary Journal and to so endow the whole as to insure an annual income of at least $30,000 from rents and money at interest for keeping up the enterprize. Correspondence with other Institutions of the kind is desired for interchange of duplicates and other Mutual benefits.
Address: Public Library of Kentucky, Louisville, Ky.
P. A. TOWNE, Librarian.

Front View of the Public Library Building, Louisville, Ky.

PUBLIC LIBRARY HALL,
FORMELY KNOWN AS
WEISIGER HALL,
is in the center of the magnificent building recently purchased by the Public Library of Kentucky and now occupied for a free Library and Museum. It is the largest, best arranged and most suitably located Hall in the City for Theatricals, Operas and public Exhibitions of every kind. The stage 40 by 45 feet with a drop Curtain 32 by 40 feet has ample scenery for all ordinary performances and beneath has a room 25 by 40 feet with the modern improvements of traps &c. The Hall is faultless in acoustics and ventilation and is so arranged that in case of fire or other accident 14 large windows along the entire northern and southern sides in addition to an enormous exit door in the western front afford prompt and easy ways of escape for the largest audience. Its location in the center of the vast Public Library building secures it from the noise of the street and it is accessible at all hours from all quarters of the City by Street rail roads. It will comfortably seat 1400 persons and by using the broad aisles and extensive lobbies has accommodated 2100. Central market heretofore held in the building is removed to Fifth Street and Public Library Hall, converted into a grand amphitheater, will soon be so enlarged, improved and adorned as to be second to none in the country. As a means of support to the Public Library and Museum which are free to everybody, the Hall is rented by the day or week or for a longer time for all respectable exhibitions and amusements. *Address: Public Library of Kentucky, Louisville, Ky.*
R. T. DURRETT, President.

Office of **Public Library of Kentucky.**

Louisville Ky. May 16 1873

In 1878, the Polytechnic Society took over the Library, bankrupt by many frivolous purchases of book, art and scientific collections.

253.

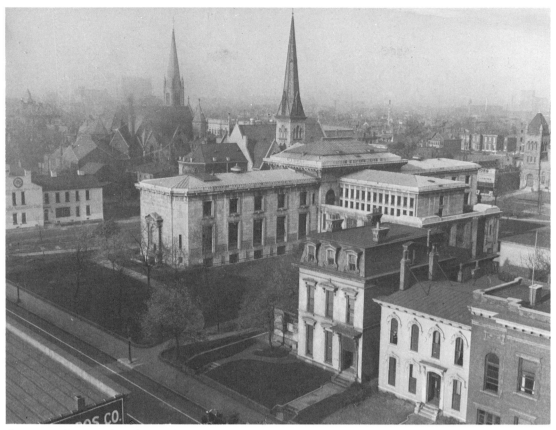

Carnegie-financed Public Library, opened in 1908, is seen from 3rd near Broadway in 1937.
254.

159.

$3.8 million Main Library Building, opened in 1969, is overlooked by 800 Bldg. on 4th St.
255.

160.

In 1867, architect John Andrewartha had envisioned a city hall with very imposing proportions, but he could build only a section of it between 1871-73.
256.

The planned completion of City Hall was blocked by the old Jail, seen in 1906.
257.

The First Christian Church, built on the N.E. corner of 4th and Walnut in 1864, stood next to Macauley's Theatre.
258.

Like most theaters of its period, Macauley's had a richly decorated interior. Opened in 1873, it could seat 1,500.
259.

162.

STUBER & BRO.,   LOUISVILLE, KY.

Country's best legitimate theater appeared at Macauley's, but
popularity waned when movie houses began to open in early 1900's.

260.

E. KLAUBER, PHOTO.   LOUISVILLE, KY.

MARY ANDERSON.

Louisville's best known actress started at Macauley's in 1875.
Movie house in her name opened in 1907 as legitimate theater.

261.

An interesting array of architectural examples are seen about 1900 adjoining Macauley's Theatre.

262.

Sign reading, "Talk Louisville and watch the Starks Building grow," indicates Macauley's demise.

263.

164.

Attendance at Female High School, finished in 1873, was normally twice that at Male.
264.

Later used by Male High, structure was incorporated into Ahrens Trade School in 1926.
265.

German Baptist Orphans' Home on E. Broadway was one of many orphanages started after the Civil War by church and fraternal groups.
266.

Masonic Widows' and Orphans' Home on 2nd between Bloom and Avery was partially opened in 1871, housed 305 when finished in 1881.
267.

166.

Earliest known view of east Main St. was published in 1855. Apparently activity is centered around residences at intersection of Brook St.
268.

Pork houses and stock yards along Beargrass Creek in Butchertown are seen from the School for the Blind on Frankfort Ave. in 1874.
269.

Station at 27th and Portland in 1874. Steam pumpers were first used when Fire Dept. started in 1858.
270.

Ca. 1875 photo of company on east side of Hancock, between Market and Jefferson, added in 1870.
271.

168.

Churchill Downs' club house, designed by City Hall architect John Andrewartha, was ready for first Derby in 1875.
272.

The Louisville Jockey Club and Driving Park Association's first grand stand was west of the club house (above).
273.

Part of the present twin-towered grand stand, built on the track's west side, can be seen at start of 1907 race.
274.

1933 Derby's stretch drive pitted Herb Fisher on Head Play (left) and the winner, Don Meade on Broker's Tip.
275.

Spectators wait patiently while the track is being watered and smoothed prior to Derby. Note infield was not crowded in early 1930's.

276.

One of the most moving moments in sports is the parade of Derby horses to the starting gate to the strains of *My Old Kentucky Home.*

277.

Arion Quartette, Louisville, 1875

Amateurs in songs for male voices.

171.

| G. W. Shaw | C. E. Wood | C. K. Needham | Louis Nahm |
| 2nd Tenor. | 1st Bass. | 1st Tenor | 2nd Bass |

172.

This photograph was made shortly after the stylish Courier-Journal Building was opened in 1876.
279.

In 1912, the newspaper moved one block east to the old Post Office at 3rd and Liberty (Green).
280.

173.

East side of 4th, south of Liberty in 1895. Statue of George Prentice sits over entrance to Courier-Journal Building.

174.

When Walter Haldeman merged his *Courier* with George Prentice's old *Journal* in 1868, Henry Watterson became editor. His penetrating editorials became the most influential published in the South.

282.

Cartoonist Thomas Nast depicted Watterson sharpening his editorial pen. Watterson served briefly in Congress during 50 years as editor of *The Courier-Journal* and was active in Democratic party.

283.

Corner pumps, made of bored pine logs, supplied drinking water; waste filled fire cisterns.
284.

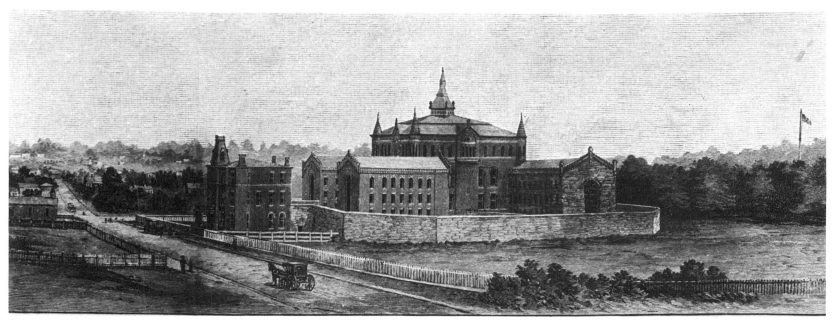

In late 1878, the Work House was opened on Payne near Lexington Rd. so inmates could break stone in the nearby quarry at Cave Hill.
285.

176.

CHAS. SHOBER & CO PROPS. CHICAGO. LITH. CO.

A. RUGER

CHURCHES.

1. First Church, Presbyterian.
2. Second   "
3. College St. Church, Presbyterian.
4. Walnut St.   "   "
5. Chestnut St.   "   "
6. Broadway Tabernacle,   "
7. Broadway Church, Methodist.
8. Walnut St.   "
9. Chestnut St.   "
10. St. Paul's Church, Episcopal.
11. St. John's   "   "
12. Christ   "   "
13. Church of Christ, Episcopal.
14. Calvary Church,   "
15. Walnut St. Church, Baptist.
16. Broadway Church,   "

17. Preston St.   "   "
18. First African   "   "
19. York St. African Church, Baptist.
20. Cathedral of the Assumption.
21. St. Patrick's Church, Roman Catholic.
22. St. John's Church,   "
23. St. Bonifacius Church, German.
24. Church of the Immac. Con., German.
25. St. Martin's Church, German.
26. St. Louis Bertrand Church, German.
27. Chapel of the Ursuline Sisters, German.
28. Church of the Messiah, German.
29. Madison St. Church,   "
30. St. Peter's Church,   "
31. St. Michael's Church, Roman Catholic.
32. St. Andrew's, Episcopal.

BIRD'S

KENT

177.

W OF

:ILLE

1876.

PUBLIC BUILDINGS, ETC.

33. Court House.	44. Fifth " "
34. City Hall.	45. Seventh " "
35. City Hospital.	46. Eighth " "
36. Custom House and Post Office.	47. Ninth " "
37. Industrial Exposition Building.	48. Tenth " "
38. Public Library of Kentucky.	49. Masonic Widows' and Orphans' Home.
39. Medical College—University of Louisville.	50. House of Refuge.
40. Male High School.	51. Nashville Depot.
41. Female " "	52. Fourteenth Street, Depot.
42. Third Ward School.	53. Short Line Depot.
43. Fourth " "	54. Narrow Guage Depot.

178.

President Hayes' reception, three weeks after riots, has never been equaled. 20,000 well-wishers attended gatherings at Galt House (above) and Exposition.

287.

When railroad workers' wages were cut in July 1877, nation recorded its worst rioting. Locally, 500 "thieves, beats and bummers" burned L.&N. office and stoned stores and residences before armed citizens restored order.

288.

The Louisville Boat Club, started in 1879, was located at the lower end of the public wharf in 1897; later it moved to upper River Rd. *179.*

289.

Ca. 1898 photograph shows the Jeffersonville ferry, Columbia, docked at bottom of 2nd St. and mail packets secured near foot of 4th.

290.

180.

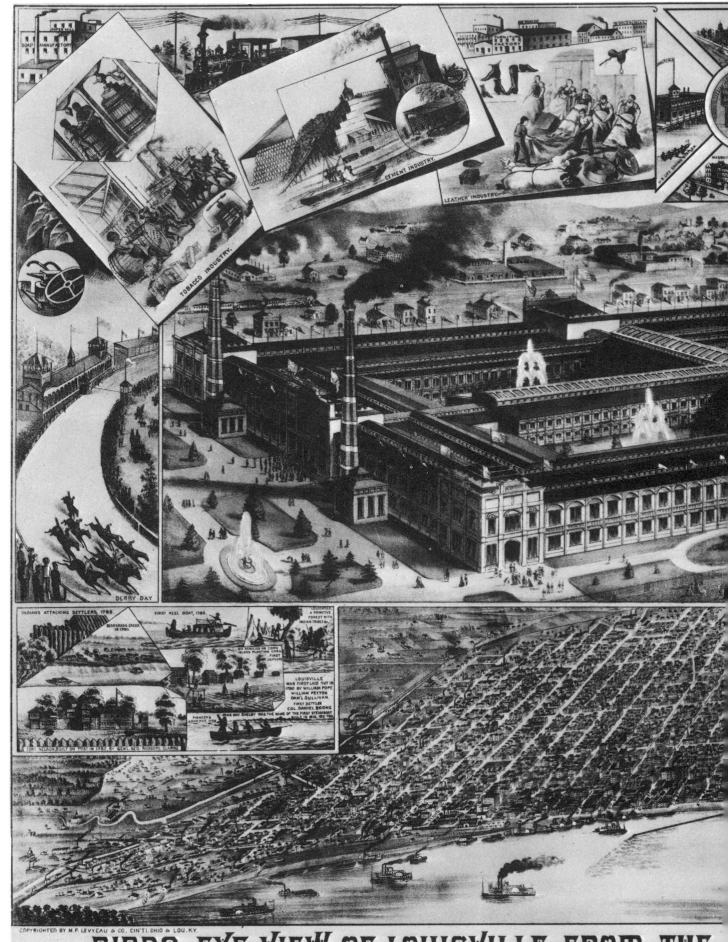

COPYRIGHTED BY M.P. LEVYEAU & CO. CIN'TI. OHIO & LOU. KY.

BIRDS-EYE VIEW OF LOUISVILLE FROM THE
DEDICATED BY THE PUBLISHERS TO THE "LOUISVI

R FRONT AND SOUTHERN EXPOSITION, 1883.
ARD OF TRADE" AND MANUFACTURING INDUSTRIES.

181.

182.

VIEW FROM THE PARK.

LOUIS
Closes

The Exposition's initial season in 1883 was so successful in attracting commerce to city, that exhibitions were continued through 188

183.

ART GALLERY AND LAKE.

displays became more commercial and less educational, exhibitions suffered financially. By 1888, land was clear for building sites.

292.

Many visitors traveled the two miles out from city on mule cars or L. & N. R.R.
293.

184.

Looking south from the DuPont estate at former site of the Southern Exposition.
294.

By 1897, St. James Court had massive homes clustered around its new fountain.
295.

The wealthy, paper-making DuPont family converted its Square into a playground years before deeding it to city in 1904 as Central Park.
296.

Outings in Central Park were once very formal affairs, as seen in 1907. Note apparel worn by the participants playing tennis at left.
297.

185.

186.

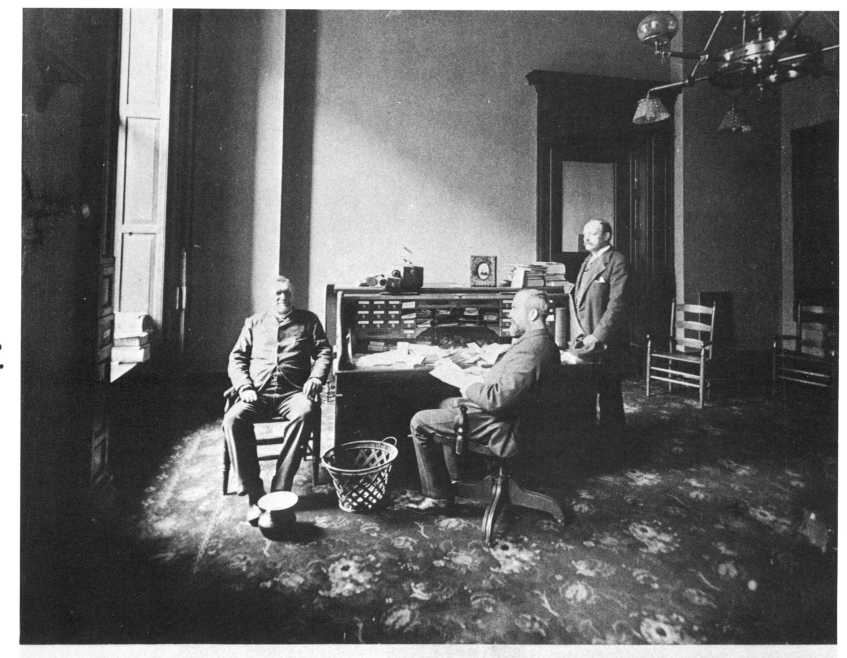

The Chief of Police, in consultation with two well known politicians.

Captioned scene was photographed about 1875. All police and firemen would continue to be political appointees for about fifty years.

298.

The dashing Louisville Police Departments of 1887 and 1889 posed intently in front of the Criminal Court Annex and City Hall (below).

299.

Before police began using automobiles in 1909, sturdy shoes were mandatory, and obviously the slang term "flatfoot" was not a misnomer.

300.

187.

188.

Between 1880-91, F. W. Mobray designed and built the Union Passenger Station at 10th and Broadway for the expanding L.&N. R. R.

An 1867 engraving shows L. & N. Railroad's first engine house near 10th and Kentucky. L. & N.'s track to Nashville was opened in 1859. **302**.

Locomotives are being serviced at L.&N. shops at 10th and Kentucky before 5 ft. gauge track was reduced to standard 4 ft. 9 in. in 1886. **303**.

Founded in 1881, the Pendennis Club was located on Walnut between 3rd and 4th before moving one block east in 1926.

304.

Germans enjoyed many diversions at the Phoenix Hill Brewery and Park at Barret and Rubel, from 1865 until 1938.

305.

Recently razed, the *ca.* 1845 Durrett home on the S.E. corner of Brook and Chestnut first housed The Filson Club, established in 1884.

306.

Editor and lawyer, Col. R. T. Durrett wrote about city's history, sometimes having "original" documents prepared to prove point.

307.

When U. of Chicago bought Durrett's library, items from former historical societies were separated for The Filson Club collection.

308.

Scene photographed during the February 1884 flood at 37th and Rudd Ave. Note dog at left, standing on roof, trying to get into window.

309.

Harper's Weekly published this 13 February 1883 scene, captioned "breaking of the embankment at Louisvi

Dog is undaunted by 1884 flood or boats being rowed across Broadway, east of Shelby St. Water is overflowing from Beargrass Creek.

310.

ly the 1937 flood caused more destruction than the series of disastrous inundations of 1882, '83 and '84.

311.

194.

In 1885, Mason Maury introduced Richardsonian, Chicago School architecture to city with his Kenyon Bldg., the first skyscraper.
312.

Massive designs and elevators allowed cornice lines to rise in the 1890's. 5th and Main to Kenyon Building is now a parking lot.
313.

Baseball was organized in Louisville in 1865. The 1885 Club posed for Stuber, with the great "Chicken" Wolf prone at right.
314.

Kentucky and Indiana Bridge, built between 1884-7, was replaced by present structure in 1913. Wybrant made photo from 33rd St. in 1886.
315.

This was fastest packet on the Ohio from completion in 1894 until destruction in 1918. It accommodated 1,500 on excursions, slept 160.
316.

Pupils at Fourth Ward School, on Walnut between Jackson and Hancock in 1887. Disciplined intellectuals have always sat on back row.
317.

Boys played marbles while girls worked out with rings on the school yard in 1920. Knickers were in style and most wore high top shoes.
318.

196.

Cartoonist Fontaine Fox (in middle) made the Brook St. mule car famous, after it was electrified in 1897, as the "Toonerville Trolley."

319.

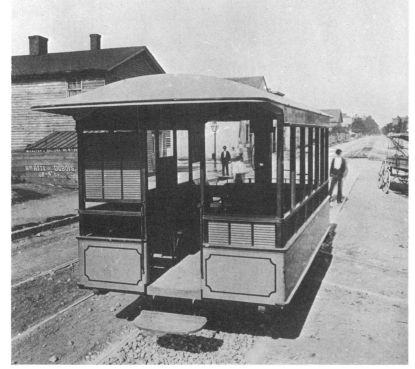

A Fourth St. to Central Park trolley in need of mules about 1875.

320.

Larger car, electrified in 1890, at Baxter and Bridge (Hamilton).

321.

198.

1889 view of Presbyterian Church on south side of Liberty between 6th and Centre (Armory).
322.

D. X. Murphy designed the sixth Jefferson County Jail which replaced the Church in 1905.
323.

Residences lining Walnut St. east of 1st in 1889 were removed when elevated North-South Expressway transected area in 1950's.

324.

199.

1889 view from City Hall shows Bull Block at 5th and Market in center, Kenyon Building at left and Galt House in upper right.

325.

200.

Now razed, the Columbia Building at 4th and Main St. epitomized the Chicago School's massive skyscraper design, popular in the 1890's.

C. J. Clarke designed old Louisville Medical College at 1st and Chestnut.

327.

1897 view of American National Bank on S.W. corner 3rd and Main.

328.

Louisville Trust Co. Bldg. on S.W. corner 5th and Market in 1897.

329.

202.

Tornado Views.
LOUISVILLE, MARCH 27TH, 1890.   15th & Chestnut Streets.   W. STUBER & BRO., Photo's.

330.

Tornado Views.
LOUISVILLE, MARCH 27TH, 1890.   10th & Market Streets   W. STUBER & BRO., Photo's.

331.

Tornado Views.
LOUISVILLE, MARCH 27TH, 1890.   9th & Main, looking west.   W. STUBER & BRO., Photo's.

332.

Tornado Views.
LOUISVILLE, MARCH 27TH, 1890.   9th & Main, looking west.   W. STUBER & BRO., Photo's.

333.

76 died as 1890 tornado cut a devastating swath from Portland to 6th St. then moved along Ohio and destroyed the Water Works' tower.
334.

Ruins at 8th and Main, included Carter Dry Goods Bldg. at right.
335.

C. J. Clarke's 1878 Carter Bldg. was enlarged when block rebuilt.
336.

204.

337.

338.

339.

340.

206.

Water was first pumped from the Ohio to a reservoir near the V.A. Hospital. In 1879, the more elevated Crescent Hill Reservoir was completed

Construction booms were different when the River Pumping Station No. 2 was being erected in 1890.

Klauber photos follow progress before tow

...ervice was restricted until a new 48" main was placed between the Crescent Hill Reservoir and the city. It is shown under construction in 1890.

341.

...en behind Works was destroyed by tornado.

343.

City's water supply was preserved after tornado although Pumping Station was isolated by flood.

344.

208.

Spectators lined 3rd St. in front of Levy Bros. early on July 4th, 1895 waiting for the parade to begin.
345.

An arch supporting a decorative lighting system frames parade's overflow crowd standing in Market St.
346.

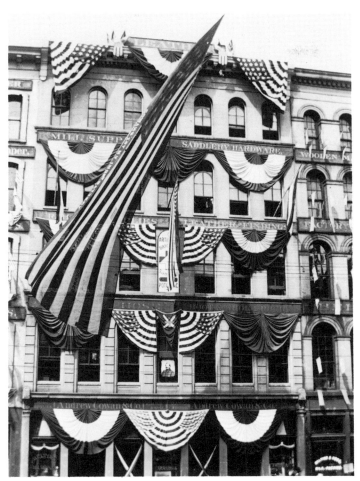

An example of Main Street's colorful decoration in 1895.
347.

Celebrations and parades were commonplace when 150,000 attended the 29th annual encampment of Grand Army of the Republic in 1895.
348.

210.

The 10-story Todd Building dominated Market St. in 1902.
349.

An 1885 Market St. landmark was the Bull Block, named for prosperous patent medicine maker, Dr. John Bull.
350.

Market Street was bustling with trolley traffic in 1907.

351.

By the 1920's, automobiles had replaced trolleys and wagons as principal mode of downtown transportation.

352.

212.

Louisville Legion, under Col. John Castleman, return from the Spanish-American War in 1898.
353.

Parades like this one about 1905, up Jefferson St. past City Hall and Courthouse, were frequent.
354.

Traffic stops on 3rd St. as police march east on Jefferson past T. P. Taylor's drug store, in 1883.
355.

When the circus arrived, as in 1909, a parade always followed. Wagons pulled caged, wild animals.
356.

Bicycles were a useful alternative to horse-drawn carriages in the late 1890's.
357.

214.

Letter carriers were mechanized for speedy delivery when photographed *ca.* 1893.
358.

Louisville Cycle Club member poses with bicycle most popular from 1870's to 1895.
359.

Base of Jefferson statue obscures Willard Hotel on Armory Place, site of new Citizens Fidelity Bank. Photograph made in late 1901.

360.

Ca. 1905 scene in front of Nic Bosler's Hotel on Jefferson St., looking down 2nd St. toward Christ Church. Note early Coca-Cola wagon.

361.

215.

Built near present Chickasaw Park, White City's roller coaster ended with splash and its operation did too, soon after opening in 1907.
362.

Children posing under Central Park's colonnade in 1907 are wearing fashionable high button shoes. Note boy working on lamp at left.
363.

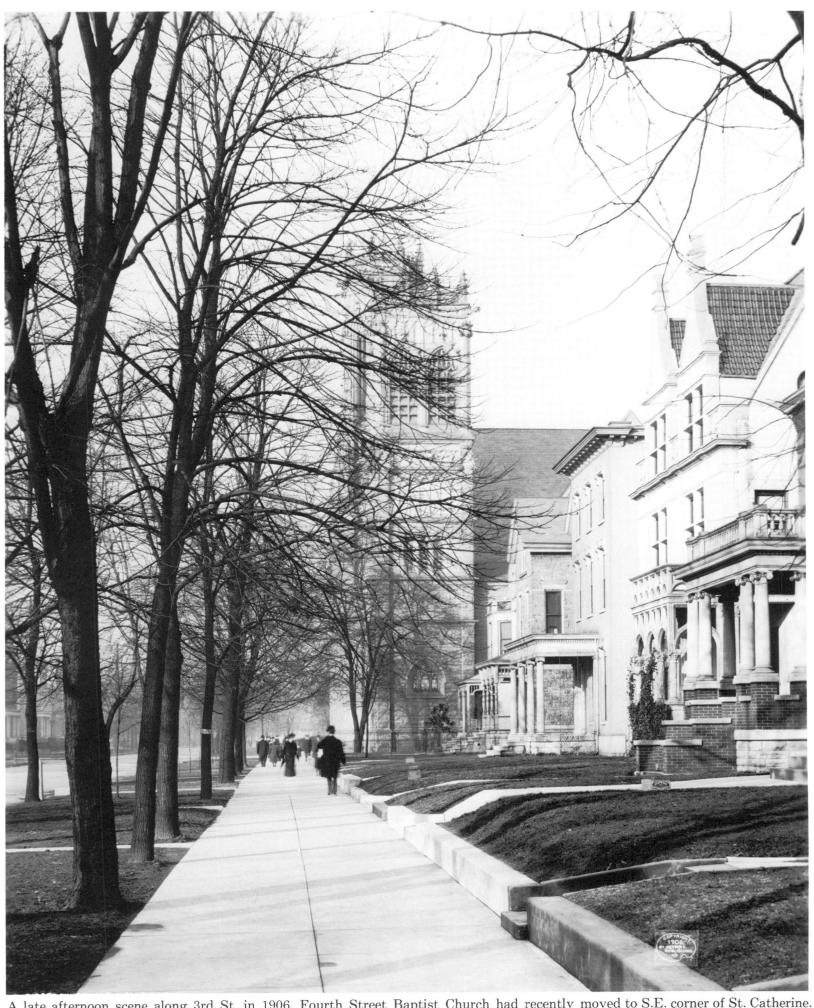

217.

A late afternoon scene along 3rd St. in 1906. Fourth Street Baptist Church had recently moved to S.E. corner of St. Catherine.

218.

Construction material still lined N. W. corner of 4th and Market when Lincoln Savings Bank opened its new office building in 1907.

365.

In 1889, Seelbach's Hotel, later the Old Inn Hotel, was on the S.W. corner of 6th and Main, east of second Louisville Hotel razed in 1950.

366.

In 1905, new Seelbach, with roof garden, opened at 4th and Walnut St.

367.

220.

Carriage houses were necessary behind homes like Samuel Culbertson's on south 3rd. *City Directory* referred to him as a capitalist.
368.

Shawnee Park provided a shady playground beside the Ohio River.
369.

Hogans provided horses in Cherokee Park with fountain in 1905.
370.

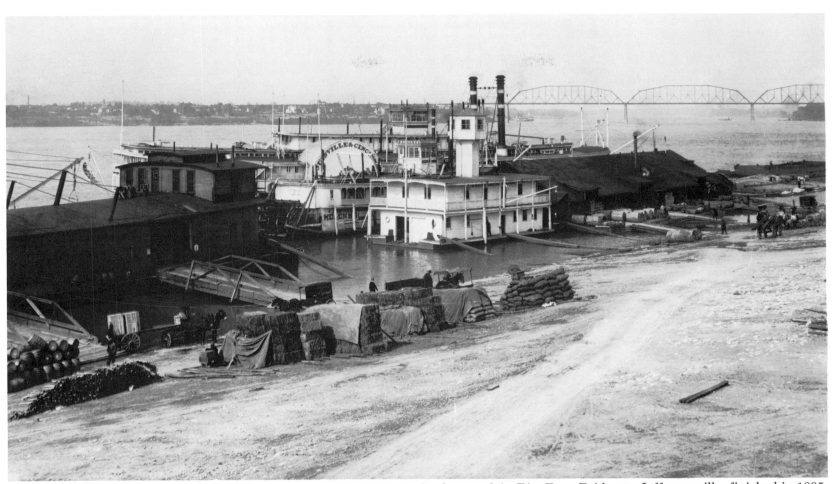

Cargo is neatly stacked on the partially paved wharf in 1907. In background is Big Four Bridge to Jeffersonville, finished in 1895.
371.

A typical stern-wheel barge proceeds down river through the Canal locks in 1906. Bridge near 28th St. leads to Shippingport houses.
372.

221.

In Dec. 1905, Courthouse roof burned. To fireproof, all interior wood was replaced by metal.
373.

In 1921, fountains and cannons ornamented Courthouse lawn. Latter were scrapped in war effort.
374.

Turn-around and ticket office of Louisville and Eastern Railroad *ca.* 1905.

375.

Terminal was on north side of Liberty east of Armory. Interurban cars went past St. Matthews, then on to LaGrange or Shelbyville.

376.

Panorama made from north side of Market between 8th and 9th, looking south. Lack of commerce on Market St. indicates photo made on a Sunday.

 224.

View from Kentucky Home Life Building shows a line of buildings along Market St. near 6th. Photograph was made during 1913 flood.

Many of the structures included in the central part of this *ca.* 1915 photograph have been destroyed and cleared by an Urban Renewal program.
377.

Residents move east on Broadway to escape flood waters of 1913. Ballard Mills was later sold by owners and the site has been cleared.
379.

Juxtaposed photos show part of amusement and exhibition areas of 1916 Kentucky State Fair.
380.

226.

40,000 attended the first officially sponsored Ky. State Fair held in 1902 at Churchill Downs.
381.

Old State Fair grounds, purchased in 1908, is now site of Miles Park. New site opened in 1956.
382.

Man on telephone pole is installing service on Belmar Dr. for Camp Taylor being built in 1918.
383.

84th Division trained on 2,730 acres north of Watterson Expwy. from Preston St. to Beargrass Cr.
384.

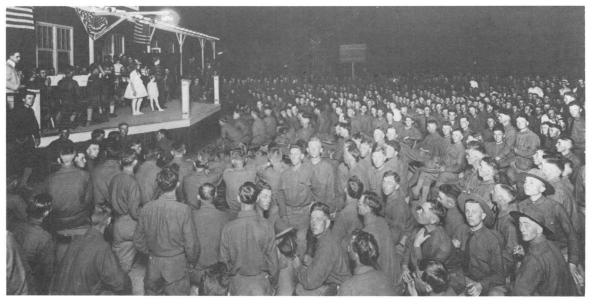

1918 flu epidemic killed 800 at Camp Taylor and 400 in Louisville. Camp was abandoned in 1920.
385.

228.

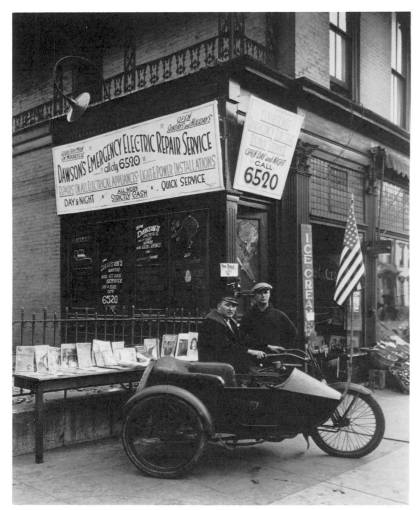

Avis Dawson operated his tiny shop at 430 W. Chestnut in 1920.
386.

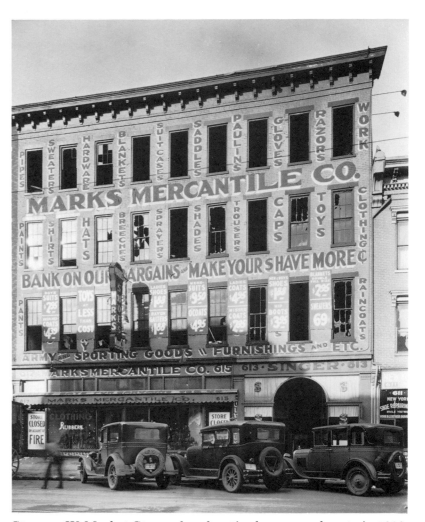

Store on W. Market St. amply advertised wares and costs in 1929.
387.

There was but one tavern and one boarding-house in the place. The boarding-house was kept by a Dr. Walter, who was also the pilot to take boats over the Falls; and he was, moreover, a great hunter and fisherman. One day in April, I think, at some public festival, several of our boarders, the leader was the Commissary of the Army, proposed to have what they called a setting, and asked me to join them. I had often heard the commissary relate his exploits — drinking egg-nog was then all the go. I declined to share in the frolic, fearing the influence of these southern blades on such occasions. . . .

It was observed one Sunday morning, soon after starting my store, that it was not opened on that day, as other establishments were; and I was asked why I kept my store closed — that Sunday had not crossed the mountains, and that I was the first person who kept his store shut on that day. I told them that I brought the Sabbath with me. It so happened that I had the honor of being the first to observe the day in Louisville.

Directly opposite to me a billiard table was kept. It was customary at the south for ladies to indulge in billiards, considering it a genteel and healthful amusement. During the morning hours, a few ladies used to honor me with a call, when I would spend a little while in that pleasant recreation; but I never gambled, and ladies' company is always more agreeable than gentlemen's. Besides, if you play with gentlemen, it is apt to lead to gambling; and it was consequently better to pay for the use of the table with ladies, when one improves in manners from their refinement.

Samuel S. Forman, 1790.

He came back from France when Tom and Daisy were still on their wedding trip, and made a miserable but irresistible journey to Louisville on the last of his army pay. He stayed there a week, walking the streets where their footsteps had clicked together through the November night and revisiting the out-of-the-way places to which they had driven in her white car. Just as Daisy's house had always seemed to him more mysterious and gay than other houses, so his idea of the city itself, even though she was gone from it, was pervaded with a melancholy beauty.

He left feeling that if he had searched harder, he might have found her — that he was leaving her behind. The day-coach — he was penniless now — was hot. He went out to the open vestibule and sat down on a folding-chair, and the station slid away and the backs of unfamiliar buildings moved by. Then out into the spring fields, where a yellow trolley raced them for a minute with the people in it who might once have seen the pale magic of her face along the casual street.

The track curved and now it was going away from the sun, which, as it sank lower, seemed to spread itself in benediction over the vanishing city where she had drawn her breath. He stretched out his hand desperately as if to snatch only a wisp of air, to save a fragment of the spot that she had made lovely for him. But it was all going by too fast now for his blurred eyes and he knew that he had lost that part of it, the freshest and the best, forever.

F. Scott Fitzgerald, [1919].

In 1923, farmers sold produce in open haymarket area on E. Market. Large sheds were added later.

388.

Woolworth's display verified its 5 and 10¢ claim. Only price of milk has not changed since 1927.

389.

230.

Crowd watches quenching of fire on south side of Market between 2nd and 3rd *ca*. 1920.

390.

Straw hats have been replaced by protective helmets and much of block has been razed.

391.

Broadway Athletic Club sponsored boxing in its open arena at 821 W. Broadway in 1920's.
392.

Crowd intently listens to lone orator on raised platform at old Fair Grounds in 1921.
393.

1927 black baptism is witnessed by many white spectators lining wharf and on the *America.*
394.

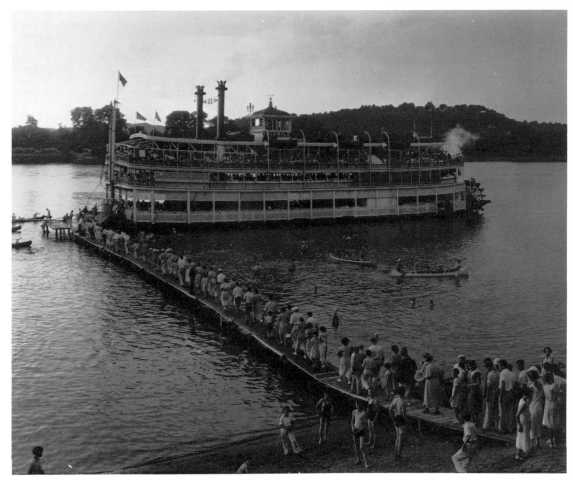

The *Idlewild,* now *Belle of Louisville,* is boarded at Fontaine Ferry Park for evening cruise.
395.

1923 view of airfield north of Taylorsville Rd. rented by A. H. Bowman and then U.S. Army. Note Crescent Hill Reservoir at top left.

396.

Confined by short runways, Bowman Field became obsolete. In 1947, Standiford Field was opened and since has been enlarged many times.

397.

234.

A well-shaded hammock afforded relaxation on summer afternoons and a respite from work in the back yard garden.
398.

A Caufield and Shook photograph finely documents a 1926 living style, when one man's best friend was a parrot.
399.

235.

One-armed bandits pose on the Courthouse steps in 1920. The slot machines were evidently confiscated in a raid.
400.

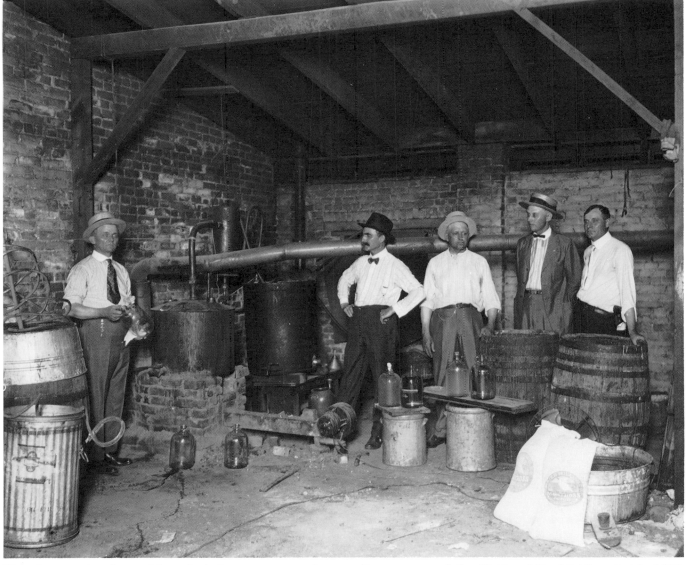

Illegal apparatus for making alcohol was uncovered soon after passage of the National Prohibition Act in 1920.
401.

236.

Solger's ice cream parlor, on N.E. corner of 4th and Broadway, was very popular.
402.

School Board recently purchased Brown Hotel which replaced Solger's in 1923.
403.

Southern Baptist Theological Seminary was still at 5th and Broadway in 1920's.
404.

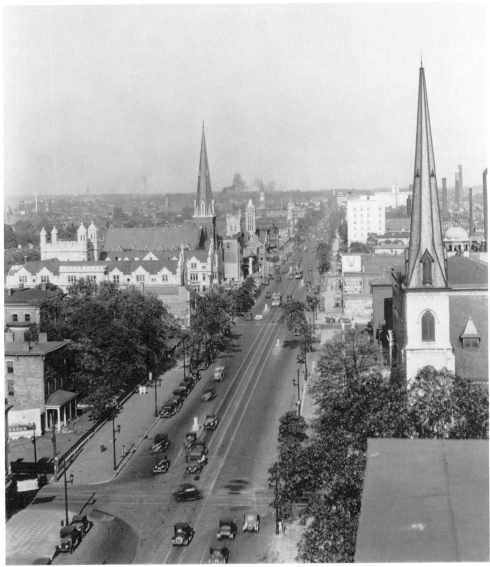

Looking east on Broadway from present site of the Portland Building, in 1927.
405.

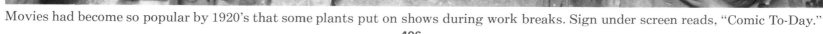

238.

Movies had become so popular by 1920's that some plants put on shows during work breaks. Sign under screen reads, "Comic To-Day."
406.

Art of chicken plucking before Colonel Sanders moved to town.
407.

Contrary to common belief, some men have been liberated from jobs.
408.

Horse-drawn ice wagon is double parked on Jefferson at 2nd in 1926.
409.

The Jefferson Meat Market would prepare venison upon special request.
410.

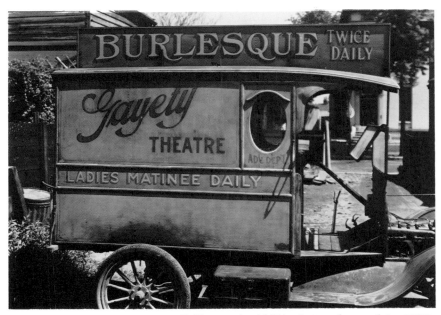

Savoy and Gayety were on Jefferson in 1920's; latter burned in 1936.
411.

240.

Almost two weeks of incessant rain in January 1937 caused an inundation which surpassed the 1883 flood in both magnitude and damage.
412.

George Bailey's photographs show extent of flooding along forks of Beargrass Creek (above) and crest of 51.7 feet compared to bridge.
413.

Red Cross provisions are being loaded into boats from high ground near the Bourbon Stock Yards.
414.

Barret Ave. pontoon bridge, buoyed by whisky barrels, linked city with dry ground of Crescent Hill.
415.

Boats lined curbs when water subsided. Reminder marked houses and cars near 23rd and Broadway.
416.

242.

Refugees leave the city by pontoon bridge over Beargrass Creek.
417.

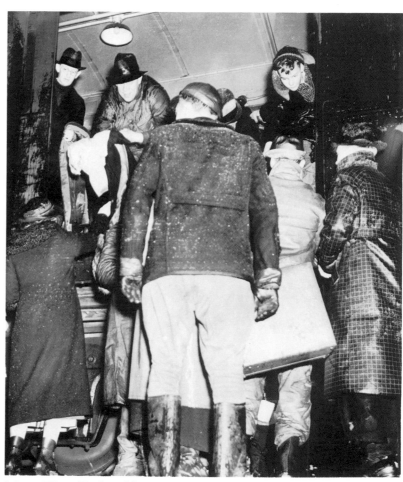

Many West End residents were evacuated by boat and then train.
418.

Streets were patrolled by Army and police to prevent looting.
419.

Pumping out Stewart's is indicative of massive clean up needed.
420.

Line of refugees wraps around corner of 12th and Broadway, patiently waiting for food and water from emergency distribution center.
421.

At same corner, Margaret Bourke-White took an award-winning photograph for *LIFE*. Dichotomy of 1930's depression is well-expressed.
422.

243.

George Rogers Clark is honored by Founders Square and its unique tourist center.
423.

Unimposing structures covered N.W. corner of 5th and Walnut before Founders Square.
424.

View from Founders Square of Rice's store, before Kentucky Hotel was built in 1925.
425.

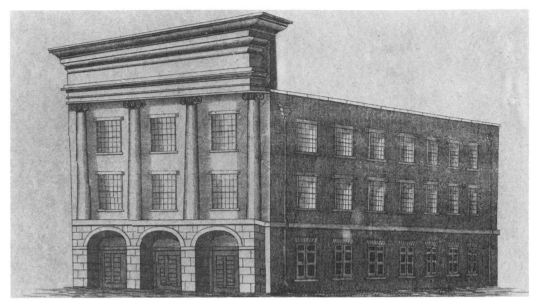

First public school was established by Mann Butler on S.W. corner of 5th and Walnut.
426.

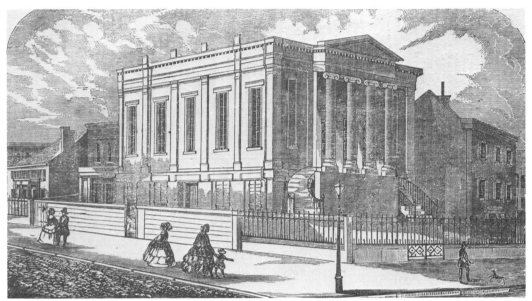

The stuccoed Walnut Street Methodist Church replaced the public school in 1853-54.
427.

National Vaudeville Theatre replaced Church about 1910. Site is a parking lot now.
428.

246.

Walnut St. west of Armory transects one of the areas cleared by Urban Renewal starting in 1962.
429.

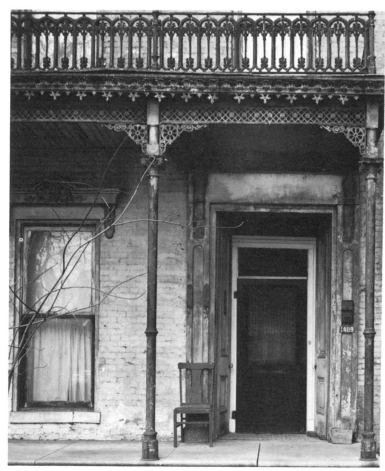

Blighted residental areas were razed for new construction.
430.

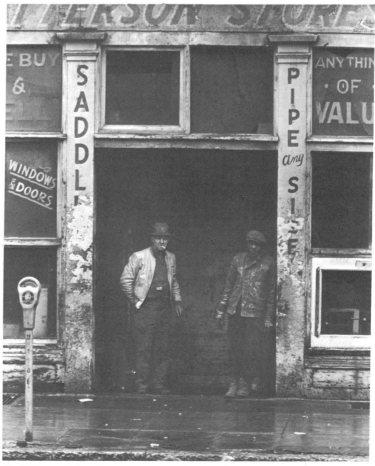

Buildings in both near east and west downtown were removed.
431.

4th and Walnut, looking north in 1906. Christian Church was replaced by the Starks Building in 1912.

432.

Retail mecca in 1926 has recently declined as Main St. did when residental areas moved further away.

433.

248.

Construction booms can be seen above river front, as bank buildings supply impetus for continued revitalization in city's oldest part.

Once bustling public wharf became a landing for an occasional paddle wheeler and a tranquil place to fish, when not a parking lot.
435.

River front takes on a new appearance as an expressway, hotel and parking garage hover over old wharf. 4th St. runs south at left.
436.

NOTES AND CREDITS

2. Glass transparency of Jefferson County Courthouse, *ca.* 1880. Owned by *The Courier-Journal • The Louisville Times.*

8. Glass transparency of Third and Jefferson St., looking south in 1888. Owned by *The Courier-Journal • The Louisville Times.*

11. Text. "Journal of an expedition along the Ohio and Mississippi by Captain Harry Gordon 1766," *Collections of the Illinois State Historical Library,* Vol. 11 (1916), pp. 290-311.

   1. William Brasier's manuscript map is in the Gage Papers, William L. Clements Library, University of Michigan, Ann Arbor.

12. 2. The Filson Club. Sketch by unknown artist probably commissioned by Col. Durrett, although in his *Centenary of Louisville . . .*, The Filson Club Publication No. 8, 1893, p. 16, he states, "among [Brooks'] papers Crayon likenesses of many of our most eminent pioneers, and drawings of a number of the early buildings of the city." The drawings are too crude to be by Brooks.

   3. The Filson Club.

   4. First announcement by Campbell and Connolly of their establishing a town at the Falls of the Ohio appeared in the *Virginia Gazette* (Dixon and Purdie), 7 April 1774, p. [3], col. [1]. Virginia State Library, Richmond.

13. 5. Painting by Frederick C. Yohn [1875-1933] "The Fall of Fort Sackville," commissioned in 1923, is owned by the Indiana Historical Bureau, Indianapolis.

   6. Miniature by George Catlin [1796-1872], dated 1832, is in the Missouri Historical Society, St. Louis. Although painted some years after Clark's death, it was copied presumably from a John Wesley Jarvis [1780-1840] portrait once owned by William Clark of St. Louis. The Clark family considered Jarvis' portrait to be the best likeness of George Rogers Clark, but unfortunately it cannot now be located.

   7. Miniature by an unknown English or Irish artist is owned by the Fogg Art Museum, Harvard University, Cambridge.

14. 8. The Filson Club. Col. Durrett had many forts and stations drawn, based upon "ground plans found among the papers of Gen. Clark." The Clark papers have been carefully researched by many scholars, but none has ever located these ground plans. The overall concept of Fort-on-Shore is perhaps reliable, but the detail is not authentic.

   9. Made by R. C. B. Thruston, 12 July 1912. The Filson Club.

Wharf was still busy in 1930. Caufield and Shook Coll., neg. 111185, Photographic Archives, U. of Louisville.

15. 10. Durrett Collection, University of Chicago Library. Corbly cannot be identified. There are two other 1779 maps of Louisville at the University of Chicago. One with the initials "CRC" [note: not G.R.C.] is attributed to George Rogers Clark. The other, similar to the Corbly map, is reportedly by William Bard. Both are undoubtedly frauds prepared by, or for, Durrett. The same hand made both maps. Close examinations of the number "7" in the dates, and the letters in Beargrass Creek on both maps confirm this. Clark is called a city designer for this plan which shows public spaces north of both Main and Liberty from 1st to 12th St. Yet the Corbly map which appears to be authentic except for the lot numbers shows available lots on both the north and south side of Main. George Rogers Clark was in Louisville only in the fall of 1779, but he makes no reference in his papers of making such a far reaching ground plan.

16. 11. Made by Dr. Ernest M. Ellison, 2 May 1971.

   12. Detroit Publishing Co. Collection, Library of Congress, neg. LC-D4-19371. Statue, executed in Rome and cast in Berlin, by Moses Ezekiel [1844-1917] was dedicated 9 November 1901.

17. 13. 1885 sketch, made for Col. Durrett. The Filson Club.

14. Made by R. C. B. Thruston, 20 June 1912. The Filson Club.

Text. Neville B. Craig, ed., "Journal of General [Richard] Butler," *The Olden Time;* . . . Cincinnati, 1876, Vol. 2, No. 11, p. 494.

   15. Engraving owned by The J. B. Speed Art Museum is one of four "American Views," executed about 1830 by engraver, James W. Steel [1799-1879] and landscape painter and lithographer, Thomas Doughty [1793-1856] of Philadelphia.

18. 16. The Library Co. of Philadelphia. General Richard Butler stated in 1786, "we passed over from the lower end to the main, to Campbell's land, thence to where he has laid out a new town called Hebron, opposite the lower part of the falls and Clarksville."

19. 17. Section of map engraved by Henry D. Pursell and printed by T. Rock at Philadelphia in 1784, owned by The Filson Club.

   18. Hand-drawn sketch on frontispiece of *Admonitions From The Dead,* . . . , London, 1754, owned by The Filson Club.

20. 19. Made by R. C. B. Thruston, June, 1923. The Filson Club.

   20. Made by R. C. B. Thruston, 22 March 1922. The Filson Club.

21. 21. The Filson Club.

22. 22. The Filson Club.

   23. Jefferson County Bond and Power of Attorney Book 1, p. 252.

Text. George P. Garrison, ed., "A Memorandum of M. Austin's Journey," *American Historical Review,* Vol. 5, No. 3 (1900), p. 527.

251.

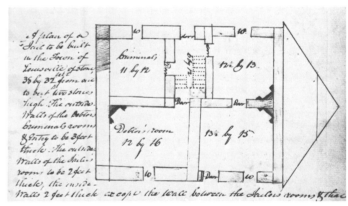

Plan of Jail built by Evan Williams in 1802-3. Jefferson County Bond and Power of Attorney Book 2, p. 163.

23. 24. *Ca.* 1890 photograph owned by The Filson Club.

   25. Made by R. C. B. Thruston, 14 October 1907. The Filson Club.

24. 26. Made by R. C. B. Thruston, 28 March 1911. The Filson Club.

   27. Made by R. C. B. Thruston, 28 March 1911. The Filson Club.

25. 28. Prints and Photographs Division, Library of Congress. William Charles [1776-1820] of Philadelphia etched caricatures of the War of 1812.

Text. Alfred Pirtle, ed., *James Chenoweth, The Story of One of the Earliest Boys of Louisville and Where Louisville Started,* Louisville, 1921, pp. 27-39.

   29. Made by R. C. B. Thruston, 9 April 1911. The Filson Club.

26. 30. Durrett Collection, University of Chicago Library. Original map was filed in Jefferson Quarter Sessions Court, chancery division case, Gray vs. Trustees of Louisville, 522 (1817). It is no longer in the suit file, but the deposition of Abraham Hite in 1814 places the establishment of lot numbers at a later date. The signatures of Hite and Breckinridge on the published map are not authentic. The style of lot numbering and printing of "Public" (top middle) appear to be of a later character found on other early maps of Louisville which Durrett probably had prepared.

27. 31. *Atlas* accompanying Victor Collot, *A Journey in North America* . . . Paris, 1826 reprinted, Florence, Italy, 1924.

   32. George Imlay, *A Topographical Description of the Western Territory of North America:* . . . , London, 1793, op. p. 51. Map may have been made before 1788 when the name of Fort Fenny [Finney] now the site of Jeffersonville, Indiana was changed to Fort Steuben.

28. 33. Made by Dr. Ernest M. Ellison, July 1968.

29. 34. Portrait by Kentucky artist, Joseph H. Bush [1794-1865] *ca.* 1817. The Filson Club.

   35. *Kentucky Gazette and General Advertiser,* Vol. 17, No. 894, 1 November 1803, p. [4], col. [4].

31.

32.

33.

34.

252.

35.

36.

37.

38.

39.

40.

41.

42.

36. *Kentucky Gazette and General Advertiser*, Vol. 17, No. 895, 8 November 1803, p. [2], col. [4].

37. National Archives, Record Group 46.

38. Male and female Hooded Mergansers, endorsed by Audubon, "Chute de L'Ohio, March 7, 1810." Harvard College Library, Cambridge. For further information on the birds Audubon painted while in Louisville see R. Haven Wiley, "Audubon's Kentucky Birds, Including the Ivory-Billed Woodpecker," *The Kentucky Warbler*, Vol. 46, No. 2 (1970), pp. 27-36.

39. Cardinal initialed "J. A." was endorsed by Audubon "Chute de L'Ohio, June 19th, 1808." The Filson Club. Audubon gave the watercolor to naturalist William C. Galt, M.D. of Louisville.

40. Passenger Pigeon signed by Audubon, endorsed, "Chute de L'Ohio, Decemb. 11, 1809." Harvard College Library, Cambridge.

41. Chimney Swallow, signed and endorsed by Audubon, "Chute de L'Ohio, July 27, 1808." Harvard College Library, Cambridge.

Text. Maria R. Audubon, ed., *Audubon and His Journals*, Dover Publications, Inc., New York, 1960. Vol. 2, pp. 486-490.

42. Crayon drawing of James Berthoud by Audubon, *ca.* 1820. The J. B. Speed Art Museum.

43. Crayon drawing of Mrs. James Berthoud by Audubon, *ca.* 1820. The J. B. Speed Art Museum.

44. One of published series, endorsed "Tarascon Mills — Shippingport, Flood at Louisville, 1883, Wybrant Photographer." The Filson Club.

45. Made by Brent Altsheler of Louisville *ca.* 1925. Altsheler Collection, University of Chicago Library. Mr. Altsheler's photographs of Louisville and Kentucky *ca.* 1925 were sold to the University of Chicago in 1941. Captain Francis McHarry was a pilot and packet owner as well as a Tarascon Mill supervisor.

46. Made prior to 1892. Copy, Caufield and Shook Collection, neg. 73764, Photographic Archives, University of Louisville.

Text. Thomas Ashe, *Travels in America, . . .* , London, 1808, pp. 236-7; Henry McMurtrie, *Sketches of Louisville . . .* , Louisville, 1819, pp. 161-163.

47. Made by Brent Altsheler *ca.* 1925. Altsheler Collection, University of Chicago Library.

48. Undated photograph in the Historic American Buildings Survey, Ky., 56-Sama, 2-1, Library of Congress. Ridgeway, restored by architect Arthur Loomis for Aubrey Cossar, is now the home of Judge and Mrs. Alex P. Humphrey.

49. The Filson Club. This is earliest view of home John Gwathmey built between 1810 and 1812 on 6th St. south of Liberty, now site of the State Office Building.

50. The Filson Club. Gwathmey operated the Union Hall at the Sign of the Indian Queen on the S.E. corner of 5th and Main from about 1805 until 1819. He is credited with planning the third County Courthouse in 1812, and supervising its construction until 1818.

Text. Henry Bradshaw Fearon, *Sketches of America . . .* , London, 1818, pp. 242-250.

51. Made by R. C. B. Thruston, 21 November 1915. The Filson Club.

52. The Filson Club.

53. Made by R. C. B. Thruston, 21 November 1915. The Filson Club.

54. *Louisville Illustrated*, H. R. Page & Co., 1889, part 2.

55. One of published series, endorsed, "Tornado Views. Louisville, March 27th, 1890. W. Stuber & Bro., Photo's." The Filson Club.

56. Owned by Locust Grove restoration, Louisville.

57. Portrait by John Wesley Jarvis [1780-1840] of New York, painted at Locust Grove, November 1820. Owned by Locust Grove restoration.

58. *Ibid.*

59. Made by R. C. B. Thruston, 21 March 1911. The Filson Club.

60. Right side prior to restoration by R. C. Thruston. The Filson Club. Left side and juxtaposition by H. Joseph Scheirich, III, made for cover of *The Register of the Kentucky Historical Society*, Vol. 65, No. 4 (1967).

61. Made by H. Joseph Scheirich, III, published in Samuel W. Thomas, "History in houses: Locust Grove, near Louisville, Kentucky," *ANTIQUES*, Vol. 41, No. 2 (1967), p. 227.

62. Section of 1819 map of Kentucky by Luke Munsell [1790-1854], owned by Kentucky Historical Society, Frankfort.

Text. W. N. Haldeman, ed., *Picture of Louisville, Directory and Business Advertiser*, Louisville, 1844, p. 50.

63. Made by R. C. B. Thruston, 1 July 1910. The Filson Club.

64. Made by R. C. B. Thruston, 1 July 1910. The Filson Club.

45.

46.

47.

48.

49.

51.

52.

53.

54.

55.

56.

57.

65. Henry McMurtrie, *Sketches of Louisville . . .* , Louisville, 1819, frontispiece. Owned by Dr. Ernest M. Ellison.

66. Portrait of Henry McMurtrie, M.D. by unknown artist, was reproduced in Franklin Spencer Edmonds, *History of Central High School*, Philadelphia, 1902.

67. Henry McMurtrie, *Sketches of Louisville*, 1819, title page.

68. The J. B. Speed Art Museum. Blue Staffordshire by Enoch Wood & Sons.

69. Richard Edwards, ed., *. . . Edwards' Directory . . . for 1867-8*, Louisville, p. 106.

70. *Ballou's Pictorial Drawing-Room Companion*, Vol. 11, 1856, p. 249.

71. *Art Work of Louisville, Kentucky*, The Charles Madison Company, Chicago, 1897, part 8.

72. Richard Deering, *Louisville, Her Commercial, Manufacturing and Social Advantages . . .* , Louisville, 1859, p. 87.

73. Jefferson County Commissioner's file, The Filson Club.

74. Reprint by Historic Urban Plans, Ithaca, New York.

75. The J. B. Speed Art Museum.

Old Louisville City Hospital on Chestnut St. about 1880. Library, *The Courier-Journal•The Louisville Times.*

76. John E. Semmes, *John H. B. Latrobe and His Times, 1803-1891*, The Norman Remington Co., Baltimore, 1917, p. 204.

77. An undated painting by G. N. Grimes of Christ Church as remembered by Alfred Pirtle in 1845. The Filson Club. J. D. Campbell, *Louisville Business Directory*, for 1864, p. 73 states "the main part of the edifice was built in 1824-5, but it has since been greatly enlarged and the interior entirely remodeled."

78. Made by William W. Bowers, undated, Bowers Collection, Photographic Archives, University of Louisville. Bowers [d. 1969] joined the Caufield and Shook firm in 1907, later became a partner. He made the first aerial photographs in Louisville.

79. American Antiquarian Society photograph of original in Museum of Natural History at Havre, France.

80. American Antiquarian Society photograph of original in Museum of Natural History at Havre, France. Lesueur made seven very vague sketches in the Louisville vicinity.

81. Richard Deering, *Louisville, Her Commercial, Manufacturing and Social Advantages . . .* , Louisville, 1859, p. 60.

Text. Bernard, Duke of Saxe-Weimer Eisenach, *Travels Through North America, During the Years 1825 and 1826*, Philadelphia, 1828, Vol. 2, p. 130.

82. "*Geological Profile* extending from *Louisville* to the *Knobs*" and "*Profile of the Louisville and Portland Canal*" were published as illustrations for the "Notice of the Louisville and Shippingport Canal, and of the Geology of the vicinity," in Benjamin Silliman, ed., *American Journal of Science and Arts*, Vol. 14, No. 1 (1828), pp. 65-69.

83. Hall Collection, Lilly Library, University of Indiana, Bloomington. Endorsed, "View of the Ohio from Shippingport near Louisville in Kentucky, looking down the River, 14th May 1828." Drawing made with a camera lucida was published with 40 others to accompany Basil Hall, *Travels in North America in the Years 1827 and 1828*, Edinburgh, 3 vols., 1829.

84. Hall Collection, Lilly Library, University of Indiana, Bloomington. Endorsed, "Study in a Forest of Kentucky, near Louisville, 10th May 1828."

85. Hall Collection, Lilly Library, University of Indiana, Bloomington. Endorsed, "A large Sycamore tree near Louisville in Kentucky, 35 feet in circumference at 5 feet from the ground, 13th May 1828."

86. Hall Collection, Lilly Library, University of Indiana, Bloomington. Endorsed, "Mr. Hunley's Country House near Louisville, Kentucky, 10th May 1828."

58.
87. Potter Collection, neg. 2441.7, Photographic Archives, University of Louisville.

59.
88. Section from 1831 map of Louisville by Hobbs (see item 91, pp. 60-61).

89. *Louisville Illustrated*, H. R. Page & Co., 1889, part 12.

90. Made by Edward Klauber in 1872. National Archives, R. G. 77-HCA-113-18P.

61.
91. The Filson Club. Map without insets was published in 1832 *Louisville Directory*.

92. For further data on Marine Hospital inset, see items 68-71, pp. 46-8.

93. For further data on Public School inset, see item 426, p. 245.

62.
Text. *History of The Ohio Falls Cities . . .*, L. A. Williams & Co., Cleveland, 1882, Vol. 1, p. 286.

94. Art Library, University of Louisville. Probably published in a German Gazeteer about 1850.

Lithograph of Louisville Hotel by Wm. Endicott of N.Y., dated 1 January 1849. Louisville Free Public Library.

63.
95. The J. B. Speed Art Museum. Drawing on stone by John H. Bufford, published by B. W. Thayer & Co. of Boston about 1845.

96. *Ca.* 1864 photograph owned by The Filson Club.

97. The J. B. Speed Art Museum. Miniature by Lawrence Sully.

64.
98. Special issue of *The Courier-Journal • The Louisville Times* entitled "Southern Property Number," 25 March 1913, Section 4, p. 1, owned by The Filson Club. Made from an 1850 photograph found under cornerstone of Masonic Temple.

99. Caufield and Shook Collection, neg. 86165, Photographic Archives, University of Louisville.

65.
100. *Art Work of Louisville, Kentucky*, The Charles Madison Company, Chicago, 1897, part 3.

101. Made by Dr. Ernest M. Ellison, May, 1971.

66.
102. *History of Second Presbyterian Church, Louisville*, 1930, p. 31.

103. Photographic copy of watercolor endorsed, "First Unitarian Church, Louisville, Ky. Drawn by J. F. C." Owned by First Unitarian Church. "J. F. C." may be the initials of James Freeman Clarke [1810-1888], minister of the Church from 1833-1840.

67.
104. Richard Edwards, ed., *Edwards' Annual Director . . . for 1864-65*, Louisville, 1864, p. 503.

105. *Ibid.* p. 75.

68.
106. John E. Semmes, *John H. B. Latrobe and His Times, 1803-1891*, Baltimore, 1917, p. 164.

69.
107. *Ibid. Ibid.*, p. 514.

108. Art Library, University of Louisville.

70.
109. *Ballou's Pictorial Drawing-Room Companion*, Vol. 11, 1856, p. 248.

70.
110. *Greater Louisville Illustrated*, National Publishing Co., Louisville, 1908, p. 75.

71.
111. Undated post card owned by Dr. Ernest M. Ellison.

112. Potter Collection, neg. 542, Photographic Archives, University of Louisville.

72.
113. Made by Dr. Ernest M. Ellison, 2 May 1971.

114. Made by Dr. Ernest M. Ellison, September 1971.

115. Made by David Talbott, 21 October 1970. Actors Theatre of Louisville.

73.
116. American Antiquarian Society, Worcester, Mass.

117. John B. Williamson, ed., *Williamson's Annual Directory of the City of Louisville, 1865 & 1866*, Louisville, 1865, frontispiece.

74.
118. By an unknown artist, attributed to Matthew Harris Jouett by the Shryock family. Kentucky Historical Society, Frankfort.

119. Undated photograph by Mathew Brady, National Archives, R. G. 111-B-1240.

Text. John Russell to W. A. J. Russell, dated 27 January 1842. John T. Flanagan, ed., "Six Letters by John Russell," *Journal of the Illinois State Historical Society*, Vol. 44, No. 1 (1951), p. 36. Another effort was made to remove the capital to Louisville in 1873.

75.
120. Lewis Collins, *Historical Sketches of Kentucky: . . .*, Cincinnati, 1847, p. 359.

121. *Art Work of Louisville, Kentucky*, The Charles Madison Company, Chicago, 1897, part 3.

76.
122. Made by Lester Jones, 26 May 1940, Historic American Buildings Survey, Ky. 56-Louvi, 4-1, Library of Congress.

123. From color slide, made by Dr. Samuel W. Thomas, September 1967.

77.
124. *The Family Magazine . . .*, Cincinnati, 1840, frontispiece.

125. Robert Sears, ed., *A New and Popular Pictorial Description of the United States*, New York, 1848, p. 483.

78.
126. The Filson Club.

127. Photograph by Mathew Brady, National Archives, R. G. 111-B-2192. Rousseau became Louisville's best-known Civil War general.

79.
128. The J. B. Speed Art Museum. Oil painting of Oakland House and Race Course was executed in 1840 by Robert Brammer and Augustus A. Von Smith, Sr.

Text. James Silk Buckingham, *The Eastern and Western States of America*, London, 1842, Vol. 3, pp. 17-35.

80.
129. Bowers Collection, Photographic Archives, University of Louisville.

130. Made in May 1928, Caufield and Shook Collection, neg. 92613, Photographic Archives, University of Louisville.

81.
131. Undated, photograph by Mathew Brady, National Archives, R. G. 111-B-1125.

132. Undated, photograph by Mathew Brady, National Archives, R. G. 111-B-1436.

82.
Text. Charles Dickens, *American Notes . . .*, London, 1842, Vol. 2, pp. 105-6.

133. The Filson Club.

83.
134. *Travelers Guide to the Louisville and Nashville Railroad*, Louisville, 1867, op. p. 25.

135. Lewis Collins, *Historical Sketches of Kentucky: . . .*, Cincinnati, 1847, p. 359.

136. *Louisville, 1861-1895, G. A. R. 29th Encampment, Souvenir and Official Programme*, Louisville, 1895, unpaged.

1845 Long Run Church burned in 1960. The Filson Club.

84.
137. Lewis Collins, *Historical Sketches of Kentucky: . . .*, Cincinnati, 1847, p. 361.

138. Broadside Collection, Rare Book Division, Library of Congress.

85.
139. *Ballou's Pictorial Drawing-Room Companion*, Vol. 11, 1856, p. 248.

140. *Art Work of Louisville, Kentucky*, The Charles Madison Company, Chicago, 1897, part 6.

253.

86. 141. The Filson Club. Engraving by Henry Sartain, Philadelphia, 1848, after a daguerreotype.

87. 142. Undated photograph owned by The Filson Club.

143. Made 8 July 1926, Caufield and Shook Collection, neg. 73957, Photographic Archives, University of Louisville.

88. 144. The Filson Club. Lithograph made and published (plate 437) by Nathaniel Currier in 1847.

89. 145. Made by R. C. B. Thruston, 19 October 1912. The Filson Club.

146. Potter Collection, neg. 3802, Photographic Archives, University of Louisville.

90. 147. Made by Detroit Publishing Co., 1906, Library of Congress, neg. LC-D4-19369.

148. *Louisville Illustrated*, H. R. Page & Co., 1889, part 3.

91. 149. Potter Collection, neg. 341, Photographic Archives, University of Louisville.

150. *Art Work of Louisville, Kentucky*, The Charles Madison Company, Chicago, 1897, part 7.

92. 151. Watercolor, entitled "Looking up the Falls of the Ohio" by an unknown artist, is owned by The J. B. Speed Art Museum.

Text. Charles Dickens, *American Notes . . .*, London, 1842, Vol. 2, pp. 100-101; Bertha L. Heilbron, ed., *With Pen and Pencil on the Frontier in 1851, The Diary and Sketches of Frank Blackwell Mayer*, Saint Paul, 1932, pp. 52-3.

93. 152. John B. Williamson, ed., *Williamson's Annual Directory of the City of Louisville, 1865 & 1866*, Louisville, 1865, op. p. 326. Stone structure later housed *The Courier-Journal•The Louisville Times*.

153. John B. Williamson, ed., *Williamson's Annual Directory of the City of Louisville, 1865 & 1866*, Louisville, 1865, op. p. 19. Another view was published in Deering's *Louisville, Her Commercial, Manufacturing and Social Advantages . . .*, Louisville, 1859, p. 68. This structure was converted into a theater in 1878 and was destroyed by fire in 1903.

94. 154. Richard Edwards, ed., *Edwards' . . . Directory . . . for 1867-8*, Louisville, 1867, op. p. 89. The Louisville Female Seminary moved to other sites beginning in 1879. Structure is opposite the old University of Louisville Medical School and has been used until recently for research laboratories.

155. Richard Deering, *Louisville, Her Commercial, Manufacturing and Social Advantages . . .*, Louisville, 1859, p. 43.

95. 156. Potter Collection, neg. 339, Photographic Archives, University of Louisville.

96. 157. Engraving, published in *Gleason's Pictorial Drawing-Room Companion* [Boston], Vol. 7, No. 9, 2 September 1854, p. 137, is owned by The J. B. Speed Art Museum.

158. Prints and Photographs Division, Library of Congress. Charles Magnus operated at the address endorsed on the letterhead after 1858, but appearances of the Fourth Street Baptist Church, and Medical School before its fire, indicate *ca.* 1855 date.

97. 159. American Antiquarian Society, Worcester, Mass. Endorsed, "Drawn by J. W. Hill. Engraved by Wellstood & Peters. Engraved by Permission for the Ladies' Repository from Views of American Cities, Published by Smith, Brothers & Co." In 1853, the *Ladies' Repository* of Cincinnati obtained permission from Smith, Brothers & Co. to re-engrave its set of larger, lithographic views. The original view of Louisville from Jeffersonville in 1850 (one is owned by The Filson Club) was republished in a much smaller version in the October, 1854 issue of the *Ladies' Repository.*

160. J. C. G. Kennedy, ed., *The Progress of the Republic, . . .*, Washington, [1856], p. 91.

98. 161. *Ibid.*, p. 72.

162. Oscar Comettant, *Voyage Pictoresque Et Anecdotique Dans Le Nord Et Le Sud Des Etats-Unis, D'Amerique*, Paris, 1866, p. 374. First edition was published in 1864. Engraving was evidently copied from one published in *James' River Guide: . . .*, Cincinnati, 1856, p. 116.

99. 163. James T. Lloyd, ed., *Lloyd's Steamboat Directory, . . .*, Cincinnati, 1856, p. 132.

164. Insert in Richard Edwards, ed., *Edwards' Annual Director . . . 1864-5*, Louisville, 1864.

101. 165. W. Lee White, ed., *Louisville City Directory, 1855-6*, Louisville, 1855, frontispiece. This is the most informative map of its period and was the first published in a city directory after 1832.

102. 166. *Ballou's Pictorial Drawing-Room Companion*, Vol. 11, 1856, p. 248.

167. Made by Detroit Publishing Co., 1907, Library of Congress, neg. LC-D4-70043.

103. 168. *Ballou's Pictorial Drawing-Room Companion*, Vol. 11, 1856, p. 249.

169. John B. Williamson, ed., *Williamson's Annual Directory of the City of Louisville, 1865 & 1866*, Louisville, 1865, p. 82 of advertisements.

James' River Guide was evidently basis for Comettant's engraving and one below owned by Dr. Donald J. Munich.

104. 170. *Ballou's Pictorial Drawing-Room Companion*, Vol. 11, 1856, p. 248.

Text. Charles Dickens, *American Notes . . . .* London, 1842, Vol. 2, pp. 101-3.

105. 171. John B. Williamson, ed., *Williamson's Annual Directory of the City of Louisville, 1865 & 1866*, Louisville, 1865, op. p. 296.

172. Caufield and Shook Collection, neg. 41100, Photographic Archives, University of Louisville.

106. 173. The Filson Club. Newspaper source is not determined.

174. *Harper's Weekly*, Vol. 1, No. 39, 26 September 1857, p. 612.

107. 175. The Speed Museum. Newspaper source is not determined.

176. *Harper's Weekly*, Vol. 1, No. 39, 26 September 1857, p. 612.

108. 177. *Frank Leslie's Illustrated Newspaper*, 13 June 1857, p. 25. View looking north near corner of Jefferson (foreground) and 6th. Building at right housed several courts and the Louisville Police Department.

178. *Harper's Weekly*, Vol. 1, No. 26, 27 June 1857, p. 408.

109. 179. Prints and Photographs Division, Library of Congress. Lithograph by Hart and Mapother of Louisville was deposited in the Clerk's Office of the District Court of Kentucky on 28 September 1859.

111. 180. Photograph of print, courtesy of Kenneth M. Newman, The Old Print Shop, Inc., New York. Lemon & Son, Inc. of Louisville owns a slightly different chromolithograph which has deteriorated in several areas. An ordinance of 27 March 1860 provided a new street numbering system beginning at First St. and working east and west. Odd numbers were on south side, even on north side. The old system started at Eighteen St. and worked east.

112. 181. Published in *Louisville Fifty Years Ago*, p. 100. Copy, Caufield and Shook Collection, neg. 46794, Photographic Archives, University of Louisville.

182. *Louisville Illustrated*, H. R. Page & Co., 1889, part 12.

113. 183. Deteriorated ambrotype is owned by The Filson Club.

184. *Art Work of Louisville, Kentucky*, The Charles Madison Company, Chicago, 1897, part 7.

115. 185. The J. B. Speed Art Museum.

116. 186. *Frank Leslie's Illustrated Newspaper*, Vol. 10, No. 254, 6 October 1860, p. 315.

187. *Frank Leslie's Illustrated Newspaper*, Vol. 11, No. 277, 16 March 1861, p. 260.

117. 188. *Louisville Past and Present: Its Industrial History . . .*, M. Joblin & Co., Louisville, 1875, op. p. 164. Photograph by Klauber.

189. *Ibid.*, op. p. 229.

190. Section of envelope, Prints and Photographs Division, Library of Congress.

254.

Hotel Preston on block shown on pp. 110-11. Potter Coll., neg. 578, Photographic Archives, Univ. of Louisville.

118. 191. *Harper's Weekly*, Vol. 5, No. 251, 19 October 1861, p. 668.

192. *Harper's Weekly*, Vol. 6, No. 263, 11 January 1862, p. 28.

119. 193. *Harper's Weekly*, Vol. 6, No. 263, 11 January 1862, p. 29.

194. By Mathew Brady, National Archives, R. G. 111-B-4326.

121. 195. *Frank Leslie's Illustrated Newspaper*, Vol. 12, No. 368, 18 October 1862, pp. 56-57.

122. 196. *Harper's Weekly*, Vol. 6, No. 302, 11 October 1862, p. 653.

197. The Filson Club. The original publication cannot be ascertained, but the engraving was republished in M. J. Wright, ed., *Official and Illustrated War Record . . .*, Washington, D.C., 1898, p. 102.

An 1858 sheet music cover for a march published by D.P. Faulds of Louisville. Collection of Martin F. Schmidt.

123. 198. *Harper's Weekly*, Vol. 6, No. 263, 11 January 1862, p. 28.

199. *Harper's Weekly*, Vol. 6, No. 303, 18 October 1862, p. 660.

124. 200. *New York Illustrated News*, Vol. 6, No. 154, 18 October 1862, p. 1.

125. 201. Insert in Richard Edwards, ed., *Edwards' Annual Director . . . 1864-5*, Louisville, 1864.

127. 202. Map of *Louisville and Its Defenses* in 1864-65, owned by Dr Ernest M. Ellison.

128. 203. Quartermaster's Department, National Archives, R. G. 165-C-1053. Items 203-207 appear to have been added as an after-thought to "Quartermaster Photographs Received from Tennessee and Kentucky, Vol. 28, pp. 156-164. None are dated. R. G. 165-C-1056 is endorsed "View of Crittenden Genl. Hospital. Erected Nov. 1864, by Capt. A. (Alba) M. (Mark) Tucker A. Q. M." Tucker may have made the other views too.

204. *Ibid.*, R. G. 165-C-1057.

205. *Ibid.*, R. G. 165-C-1056.

129. 206. *Ibid.*, R. G. 165-C-1055.

207. *Ibid.*, R. G. 165-C-1054.

130. 208. Falls area scene appeared in group listed as "The War in Kentucky-In and about Paducah, sketched by J. C. Beard and Bill Travis" in *Harper's Weekly*, Vol. 5, No. 252, 26 October 1861, p. 684.

209. "Iron-clads passing Louisville Falls at high water on the Ohio," appeared in *Harper's Weekly*, Vol. 10, No. 488, 5 May 1866, p. 281.

Text. Paper. "Reminiscences of Louisville," dated 1 March 1917, read by Alfred Pirtle before The Filson Club.

131. 210. Tintype miniature owned by The Filson Club.

133. 211. The J. B. Speed Art Museum.

135. 212. Lithograph owned by The J. B. Speed Art Museum. Another print is on display in the Social Male Chorus Hall, Louisville.

136. 213. Undated photograph by Levin Handy, Brady-Handy Collection, Library of Congress, neg. BH-826-31346.

214. Made by Dr. Ernest M. Ellison, August, 1971.

137. 215. Made by Detroit Publishing Co., 1906, Library of Congress, neg. LC-D4-19367.

138. 216. *Thirteenth Annual Report of the Louisville House of Refuge, . . . 1878*, Louisville, 1879, frontispiece.

217. *Louisville Illustrated*, H. R. Page & Co., 1889, part 12.

139. 218. *Thirteenth Annaul Report of the Louisville House of Refuge, . . . 1878*, Louisville, 1879, frontispiece.

219. Caufield and Shook Collection, neg. 95819, Photographic Archives, University of Louisville.

220. Made by Roberts, 12 March 1930. The Filson Club.

140. 221. *Travelers Guide to the Louisville and Nashville Railroad*, Louisville, 1867, op. p. 25.

141. 222. Caufield and Shook Collection, neg. 39467, Photographic Archives, University of Louisville.

142. 223. *Louisville Illustrated*, H. R. Page & Co., 1889, part 11. Congregation now Adath Israel.

224. The Filson Club.

143. 225. Collection of Martin F. Schmidt.

144. 226. The Filson Club.

227. Altsheler Collection, University of Chicago Library.

145. 228. Prints and Photographs Division, Library of Congress.

146. 229. Prints and Photographs Division, Library of Congress.

230. Prints and Photographs Division, Library of Congress.

147. 231. Detroit Publishing Co. Collection, Library of Congress, neg. LC-D4-19373.

232. Detroit Publishing Co. Collection, Library of Congress, neg. LC-D4-19374.

148. 233. Richard Edwards, ed., *Edwards' . . . Directory . . . for 1870*, Louisville, 1870, op. p. 484.

234. William Cullen Bryant, ed., *Picturesque America; . . .*, New York 1874, Vol. 2, op. p. 165.

149. 235. Photograph, probably by Edward Klauber, in the Corps of Engineer Collection, National Archives, R. G. 77-HCS-151aF. Photograph was basis for view later published by Charles Magnus in "100 Panoramic Views of American Scenes and Cities."

236. Library of Congress, LC-USZ62-10913.

150. 237. Made by Klauber, 1871, Corps of Engineer Collection, National Archives, R. G. 77-HCA-113-5P.

238. Made by Klauber, 1873, Corps of Engineer Collection, National Archives, R. G. 77-HCA-113-23P.

239. Made by Klauber, 1871, Corps of Engineer Collection, National Archives, R. G. 77-HCA-113-6P.

151. 240. Made by Detroit Publishing Co. 1906, Library of Congress, neg. LC-D4-19362.

241. Caufield and Shook Collection, neg. 45939, The Filson Club.

153. 242. Made by Klauber in 1873, Corps of Engineer Collection, National Archives, R. G. 77-HCA-113-20P. Endorsed, "View of coffer dam, derricks, and boiler boats. Excavation of rock reef along apron dam at the head of the Louisville & Portland Canal."

154. 243. Prints and Photographs Division, Library of Congress.

244. Edward King, *The Great South . . .* , Hartford, 1875, p. 697.

245. The Filson Club. Sketch made in 1872, source is not determined.

155. 246. Detroit Publishing Co., Library of Congress, neg. LC-D4-19376.

256.

U.S. Custom House and Post Office being razed in late 1942. Files of *The Courier-Journal•The Louisville Times.*

156. 247. Art Library, University of Louisville. Engraving from a sketch by George Kerr, Jr. published in *Harper's Weekly* reportedly in 1873.

248. *Every Saturday,* 29 April 1871, p. 397.

249. *Souvenir of . . . Louisville, Ky. . . . ,* Louisville, 1902, unpaged.

157. 250. L. Stierlin, *Der Staat Kentucky und die Stadt Louisville,* Louisville, 1873, frontispiece.

251. *Art Work of Louisville, Kentucky,* The Charles Madison Company, Chicago, 1897, part 5.

158. 252. *Frank Leslie's Illustrated Newspaper,* 24 October 1874, p. 109.

253. Letterhead owned by the Louisville Free Public Library.

1865 *Directory of . . . Louisville* engraving of Odd Fellows Hall on north side of Jefferson between 1st and 2nd.

159. 254. Made by R. C. B. Thruston, 18 April 1937, The Filson Club.

255. Made by R. C. Fuller, 23 September 1971, *The Courier-Journal•The Louisville Times.*

160. 256. *The Daily Graphic* [New York], 21 October 1873, p. 784.

257. Detroit Publishing Co. Collection, Library of Congress, neg. LC-D4-19365.

161. 258. Adolph Wittemann, ed., *Souvenir of Louisville, Ky.,* New York, 1906, unpaged.

259. *Art Work of Louisville, Ky.,* The Gravure Illustration Co., Chicago, 1903, part 6, p. 3.

162. 260. Macauley Collection, Photographic Archives, University of Louisville.

261. *Ibid.*

163. 262. Potter Collection, neg. 834.1, Photographic Archives, University of Louisville.

263. Caufield and Shook Collection, neg. 66471, Photographic Archives, University of Louisville.

164. 264. *Art Work of Louisville, Kentucky,* The Charles Madison Company, Chicago, 1897, part 2.

265. Caufield and Shook Collection, neg. 72001, Photographic Archives, University of Louisville.

165. 266. *Louisville Illustrated,* H. R. Page & Co., 1889, part 8.

267. *Louisville Illustrated,* H. R. Page & Co., 1889, part 3.

166. 268. Eli Bowen, *Rambles in the Path of the Steam-Horse,* Philadelphia, 1855, p. 411.

269. William Cullen Bryant, ed., *Picturesque America; . . . ,* New York, 1874, Vol. 2, p. 164.

167. 270. Potter Collection, neg. 506, Photographic Archives, University of Louisville.

271. Kentucky Room, Louisville Free Public Library.

168. 272. Original photograph was owned by Horace Taylor, Louisville. A copy is in the Potter Collection, neg. 409.1, Photographic Archives, University of Louisville.

273. *Louisville Illustrated,* H. R. Page & Co., 1889, part 7.

Klauber photo inside Southern Exposition of cottage erected by Swiss colonists in Kentucky. The Filson Club.

169. 274. Detroit Publishing Co., Library of Congress, neg. LC-D4-19986.

275. Made by Wallace Lowry, Library, *The Courier-Journal•The Louisville Times.*

170. 276. Library, *The Courier-Journal•The Louisville Times.*

277. *Ibid.*

171. 278. Kentucky Room, Louisville Free Public Library.

172. 279. The Filson Club.

280. Potter Collection, neg. 599, Photographic Archives, University of Louisville.

173. 281. Adolph Wittemann, ed., *Louisville Illustrated,* New York, 1895, unpaged.

174. 282. The Filson Club.

283. *Harper's Weekly,* Vol. 22, No. 1120, 15 June 1878, p. 1. Thomas Nast was first to characterize Republicans and Democrats as elephants and donkeys.

175. 284. Edward King, *The Great South . . . ,* Hartford, 1874, p. 695.

285. *The City of Louisville and a Glimpse of Kentucky,* Louisville, 1887, p. 13.

177. 286. Geography and Map Division, Library of Congress.

178. 287. *Harper's Weekly*, Vol. 21, No. 1084, 6 October 1877, p. 788.

288. Allan Pinkerton, ed., *Strikers, Communists, Tramps and Detectives*, New York, 1878, op. p. 384.

179. 289. *Art Work of Louisville, Kentucky*, The Charles Madison Company, Chicago, 1897, part 4.

290. Potter Collection, neg. 228, Photographic Archives, University of Louisville.

181. 291. Geography and Map Division, Library of Congress.

183. 292. Prints and Photographs Division, Library of Congress.

184. 293. Caufield and Shook Collection, neg. 110129, Photographic Archives, University of Louisville.

294. *Art Work of Louisville, Kentucky*, The Charles Madison Company, Chicago, 1897, part 9.

295. In series on the Du Pont House, The Filson Club.

185. 296. *Louisville Illustrated*, H. R. Page & Co., 1889, part 2.

297. Detroit Publishing Co., Library of Congress, neg. LC-D4-70044.

Odd collection of chairs surround dining room table in DuPont home at Central Park, *ca.* 1890. The Filson Club.

186. 298. The Filson Club.

187. 299. Kentucky Room, Louisville Free Public Library.

300. *Ibid.*

Views of L. & N. Railroad yard. Coll. of George H. Yater.

188. 301. Detroit Publishing Co. Collection, Library of Congress, neg. LC-D4-19377.

302. *Travelers Guide to the Louisville and Nashville Railroad*, Louisville, 1867, op. p. 42.

189. 303. Photograph (neg. 1437) supplied courtesy of the News Bureau, Public Relations Dept., Louisville and Nashville Railroad, Louisville.

190. 304. Made by Detroit Publishing Company, 1906, Library of Congress, neg. LC-D4-19375.

305. Copy negative in *The Courier-Journal•The Louisville Times* files.

191. 306. The Filson Club.

307. The Filson Club.

308. *Louisville Illustrated*, H. R. Page & Co., 1889, part 10.

192. 309. The Filson Club.

193. 310. The Filson Club.

311. *Harper's Weekly*, Vol. 27, No. 1367, 3 March 1883, pp. 136-7.

194. 312. *Louisville Illustrated*, H. R. Page & Co., 1889, part 9.

313. Potter Collection, neg. 2852, Photographic Archives, University of Louisville.

314. Kentucky Room, Louisville Free Public Library.

195. 315. The Filson Club.

316. Glass negative owned by the Howard Steamboat Museum, Jeffersonville, Indiana.

196. 317. Kentucky Room, Louisville Free Public Library.

318. Caufield and Shook Collection, neg. 35718, Photographic Archives, University of Louisville.

197. 319. Potter Collection, neg. 608.3, Photographic Archives, University of Louisville.

320. The Filson Club.

321. Caufield and Shook Collection, neg. 37786, Photographic Archives, University of Louisville.

198. 322. The Filson Club.

323. Made by R. C. Fuller, 28 September 1971, *The Courier-Journal•The Louisville Times*.

199. 324. *Louisville Illustrated*, H. R. Page & Co., 1889, part 4.

325. *Ibid.*, part 1.

200. 326. Made by Detroit Publishing Co., 1906, Library of Congress, neg. LC-D4-19366.

201. 327. *Art Work of Louisville, Ky.*, The Gravure Illustration Co., Chicago, part 9, p. 7.

328. *Art Work of Louisville, Kentucky*, The Charles Madison Company, Chicago, 1897, part 6.

329. *Ibid.*, part 2.

202. 330. The Filson Club. William G. Stuber [1864-1959] published several series of tornado views in 1890. He worked in Louisville from 1880-1894, then moved to Rochester, N.Y. to work for Eastman Kodak. Stuber succeeded George Eastman as president, later was chairman of the board. Unfortunately few of his photographs are extant.

331. The Filson Club.

293. 332. The Filson Club.

333. The Filson Club.

204. 334. Edward Klauber also published a series on the tornado's destruction, *Louisville, Ky. after the Cyclone*, Louisville, 1890, unpaged.

335. "Views of Cyclone," by Klauber. 1890, Library of Congress.

336. Brown-Doherty Collection, neg. 336, Photographic Archives, University of Louisville.

205. 337. Tornado views, items 337-340, were published as stereographs by George Barker, New York. Library of Congress.

338. *Ibid.* Scene in front of Baxter Square.

339. *Ibid.* Shed is being removed to uncover buried railroad car at Union Depot.

340. *Ibid.* View of destruction on Market Street.

206. 341. Items 341-344 are in an album showing the building of the pumping station in 1890. Album was prepared for Charles Mulkoy, Louisville. Photographs were probably made by Klauber. Album is owned by Mrs. Henry McElwain.

342. *Ibid.*

207. 343. *Ibid.*

344. *Ibid.*

208. 345. Potter Collection, neg. 1029, Photographic Archives, University of Louisville.

346. Cooper Collection, neg. 3, Photographic Archives, University of Louisville. The Cooper Collection glass negatives came from The Bush-Krebs Co., most being the personal work of Bush.

209. 347. Cooper Collection, neg. 6, Photographic Archives, University of Louisville.

348. Cooper Collection, neg. 2, Photographic Archives, University of Louisville.

210. 349. *Souvenir of . . . Louisville, Ky. . . . ,* Chas. T. Dearing, Louisville, 1902, unpaged.

350. Adolph Wittemann, ed., *Louisville Illustrated,* New York, 1895, unpaged.

211. 351. Made by Detroit Publishing Co., 1907, Library of Congress, neg. LC-D4-70039.

352. Caufield and Shook Collection, neg. 102198, Photographic Archives, University of Louisville.

212. 353. Made by Doerr, 1898, The Filson Club.

354. Potter Collection, neg. 681.1, Photographic Archives, University of Louisville.

213. 355. Copy negative, *The Courier-Journal•The Louisville Times* files.

356. Potter Collection, neg. 684, Photographic Archives, University of Louisville.

214. 357. *Louisville Pictorial Souvenir,* Louisville Pictorial Souvenir Company, Louisville, undated, unpaged.

358. The Filson Club.

359. Potter Collection, neg. 4034.1, Photographic Archives, University of Louisville.

215. 360. Cooper Collection, neg. 220, Photographic Archives, University of Louisville.

361. Potter Collection, neg. 936, Photographic Archives, University of Louisville.

216. 362. Made by Detroit Publishing Co., 1907, Library of Congress, neg. LC-D4-70038.

363. *Ibid.,* neg. LC-D4-70037.

217. 364. Made by Detroit Publishing Co., 1906, Library of Congress, neg. LC-D4-19359.

218. 365. *Ibid.,* LC-D4-70046.

219. 366. *Louisville Illustrated,* H. R. Page & Co., 1889, part 4.

367. Made by Detroit Publishing Co., 1907, Library of Congress, neg. LC-D4-70041.

220. 368. Photograph by Klauber owned by Dr. William F. Furnish.

369. *Year Book* [*1918*] *of the Board of Park Commissioners,* 1919, p. 5.

370. Made by Detroit Publishing Co., 1907, Library of Congress, neg. LC-D4-70045.

221. 371. *Ibid.,* neg. LC-D4-70035.

372. *Ibid.,* neg. LC-D4-19364.

222. 373. Copy negative, *The Courier-Journal•The Louisville Times* files.

374. Caufield and Shook Collection, neg. 36572, Photographic Archives, University of Louisville.

223. 375. Cooper Collection, neg. 262, Photographic Archives, University of Louisville.

376. Collection of George H. Yater.

224. 377. Prints and Photographs Division, Library of Congress.

378. Made by R. C. B. Thruston, 1 April 1913, The Filson Club.

225. 379. *Ibid.*

226. 380. Made by Caufield and Shook, 1916, Prints and Photographs Division, Library of Congress. Photograph made in three parts, only parts of two are reproduced.

381. Made by George Bailey, 14 September 1948, *The Courier-Journal• The Louisville Times.*

382. *Ibid.*

227. 383. Made by Hesse, 24 June 1918, National Archives, R. G. 165-WW-529E-5.

384. Made 26 November 1918, National Archives, R. G. 165-WW-529E-1.

385. Made by Caufield and Shook, 14 August 1918, National Archives, R. G. 165-WW-529E-4.

228. 386. Caufield and Shook Collection, neg. 33412, Photographic Archives, University of Louisville.

387. *Ibid.,* neg. 98986.

Text. Lyman C. Draper, ed., *Narrative of a Journey Down The Ohio and Mississippi in 1789-90.* By Maj. Samuel S. Forman . . . , Cincinnati, 1888, pp. 40-41; F. Scott Fitzgerald, *The Great Gatsby,* New York, 1925, pp. 152-3.

Parade made about 1918 was probably for a war related cause. *The Courier-Journal•The Louisville Times files.*

229. 388. Caufield and Shook Collection, neg. 49990, Photographic Archives, University of Louisville.

389. *Ibid.,* neg. 82463.

230. 390. Copy negative, *The Courier-Journal•The Louisville Times* files.

391. Caufield and Shook Collection, neg. 74481, Photographic Archives, University of Louisville.

231. 392. *Ibid.,* neg. 37272.

393. *Ibid.,* neg. 38333.

232. 394. *Ibid.,* neg. 85419.

395. *Ibid.,* neg. 133150.

Shop class about 1920. Caufield and Shook Coll., neg. 36794, Photographic Archives, University of Louisville.

233. 396. Made by Robert Gast, 11 April 1923. Collection of R. Fairleigh Lussky.

397. Made by James N. Keen, 24 February 1955.

234. 398. Cooper Collection, neg. 205, Photographic Archives, University of Louisville.

399. Caufield and Shook Collection, neg. 74895, Photographic Archives, University of Louisville.

235. 400. *Ibid.,* neg. 31332.

401. *Ibid.,* neg. 32546.

236. 402. *Ibid.,* neg. 46871.

403. *Ibid.,* neg. 53960.

237. 404. *Ibid.,* neg. 87025.

405. *Ibid.,* neg. 85415.

238. 406. *Ibid.,* neg. 47085.

407. *Ibid.,* neg. 74745.

408. *Ibid.,* neg. 29962.

239. 409. *Ibid.,* neg. 73819.

410. Potter Collection, neg. 561, Photographic Archives, University of Louisville.

411. Caufield and Shook Collection, neg. 31908, Photographic Archives, University of Louisville.

240. 412. Made by George Bailey, January 1937, *The Courier-Journal• The Louisville Times.*

Integrated streetcar in 1929. Caufield and Shook Coll., neg. 104424, Photographic Archives, U. of Louisville.

241.

413. *Ibid.*
414. *Ibid.*
415. *Ibid.*
416. *Ibid.*

242.

417. *Ibid.*
418. *Ibid.*
419. National Archives, R. G. 69-N-3631.
420. Made by George Bailey, January, 1937, *The Courier-Journal•The Louisville Times.*

243.

421. *Ibid.*, 8 February 1937.
422. Made by Margaret Bourke-White, 1937, *LIFE* Magazine © *Time Inc.* The 8 February 1937 issue of *LIFE* published other flood photographs on pp. 16, 17, 48, and 49.

244.

423. Made by Dr. Ernest M. Ellison, 8 October 1971.
424. Caufield and Shook Collection, neg. 83319, Photographic Archives, University of Louisville.
425. Potter Collection, neg. 450, Photographic Archives, University of Louisville.

245.

426. Inset, Hobbs' 1832 map of Louisville, The Filson Club.
427. Richard Deering, *Louisville, Her Commercial, Manufacturing and Social Advantages . . .* , Louisville, 1859, p. 24. Engraving was also published in later city directories.

428. Potter Collection, neg. 2894, Photographic Archives, University of Louisville. The church was removed at some period before the National Theatre was built in 1913. The theatre was razed in 1952.

246.

429. Made by Marion Post Wolcott, May 1840, for the Farm Security Administration. Library of Congress, neg. LC-USF34-53756.
430. Market Street scene made by H. Joseph Scheirich, III, 1966.
431. *Ibid.*

247.

432. Detroit Publishing Co. Collection, Library of Congress, neg. LC-D4-19361.
433. Caufield and Shook Collection, neg. 70659, Photographic Archives, University of Louisville.

259.

Police manually change traffic signals at 4th and Chestnut in 1927. National Archives, R. G. 306-NT-943L-1.

248.

434. Made by Billy Davis, 1 May 1971, *The Courier-Journal•The Louisville Times.*

249.

435. Made by Marion Post Walcott, July 1940, for the Farm Security Administration. Library of Congress, neg. LC-USF34-55332.
436. Made by C. Thomas Hardin, April 1971, *The Courier-Journal• The Louisville Times.*

River front from *Harper's Weekly,* 27 June 1857, p. 409.

Earliest known photograph showing north side of Main at 4th St. was taken in 1850. Collection of Thomas A. Stuebling, Jeffersontown.

INDEX

264.

Front end paper: R. C. Ballard Thruston, 11 October 1914, The Filson Club.

Back end paper: Billy Davis, 28 July 1971.

Dust cover design: Osmond S. Guy.